TO:
Dolores Curran
who first encouraged me . . .
and
my Montana writer friends
who kept it up.

To Connie
Best wishes
Happy Trails
6-7-9
Gwen Petersen

GWEN PETERSEN

THE GREENHORN'S GUIDE TO THE WOOLLY WEST

PART IV. **WOOLLY WEST RECREATION AND SOCIAL PURSUITS** or WHOOPING IT UP AT THE GIDDY-YUP CORRALS

PART V. **WOOLLY WEST COMMUNITY ACTIVITIES** or WHAT TO DO IN THE WILDERNESS

INTRODUCTION

THE GREENHORN'S GUIDE
TO THE WOOLLY WEST

(A Manual of Do's and Don'ts for the Western Tenderfoot)

by

Gwen Petersen

This book has been compiled to meet a crying need. The crying can be heard throughout the Western States issuing in wails from the throats of those new pioneers who followed their fantasies and moved OUT WEST.

Lots of folks have moved OUT WEST. Possibly including you. Rich, poor, or in between, you've found that little nest somewhere out in the West. Maybe you are affluent enough to have purchased an actual full-sized ranch complete with live-in cowboys and dogies. (Dogies: pronounced to rhyme with doughgeez. It's a term mostly obsolete except in songs and movies and refers to four footed creatures that give beef.)

Perhaps you're a person of modest means who purchased a few acres near a small town where you planned to raise some chickens and your kids could have a horse.

Possibly you've retired from your job or profession and you've wagon-trained OUT WEST intending to spend your twilight years in the quiet atmosphere of a small town where life is simple and folks are down to, and the salt of, the earth.

Perchance you're a young person or couple who arrived by thumb or van. You owned a backpack, good health and the highest of ideals. Your goal was to live with nature, grow your own food, avoid contamination by this oh-so-plastic society and become totally self-sufficient. So you begged a rancher to rent you an old homestead shack that has no indoor plumbing and now you tan hides for a living.

It could be you're someone who fulfilled a fantasy by trekking OUT WEST on your vacation to a dude ranch where you got to call one horse "yours" for two weeks.

Whatever your background, this manual for the tenderfoot offers guidance and counseling to the eager Greenhorn (defined in Webster as a "raw, inexperienced person") who yearns to become part of the high, wide and handsome land of cowgirls and cowboys.

In my own Greenhorn days, I was fortunate enough to have Frances, a born and bred Western friend, who undertook to initiate me into the Ways of the Woolly West. Shouldering her responsibility with vigor, dedication and deadpan verve, she spent uncounted hours devising fresh schemes that often deteriorated into hilarious fiascos— which she claimed were unintentional.

As Frances always said, "No matter where you hail from or who you think you are, there's plenty of room OUT WEST for whoopin' 'n hurrahin'."

PART I

WHEN THE WAGON TRAIN HALTS

DON'T PANIC, MOST WESTERNERS SPEAK SOME ENGLISH

CHAPTER 1

DRESS CODE OF THE WEST

(After walking-tall boots, 20-gallon hats, moseyin' jeans and a down-filled vest, what is there under heaven?)

Before I arrived in the Woolly West, I knew exactly what the rugged Western male wore . . . a rafter-high hat and denim jeans cut admirably high in the crotch, with

pantlegs stuffed inside shin-tall, high-heeled boots incised with yellow butterflies. I knew that strong, silent Tall-
in-the-Saddle kept his eyes slitted, his expression con-
templative above firm jaw, and that he stalked around slapping leather. Out West, slapping leather is not a questionable sexual practice. It's a smacking sound made when
the hand hits the holster during a quick draw.

Besides big hats and high heeled boots, I was positive
that a cowboy wore a sweat-stained leather vest with a
pocket where he carried his "makin's ."("Makin's" include a drawstring cotton pouch full of Bull Durham
tobacco bits and a packet of cigarette papers.) To watch a
true cowboy standing proud in hat, vest, jeans, boots,
spurs and chaps—pronounced shaps—while he finger-
furrows a tissue-thin oblong of paper, flicks flakes of
tobacco onto it, draws the pouch string closed with his
teeth, leaves it dangling there while he rolls the paper
around the tobacco forming a tube, then licks the edge
before sealing and finally snicks a kitchen match with a
thumbnail to light the results, is to have a religious experience. Cowboys who don't smoke, chew. (See chapter
on chewing.)

Of course, I knew too that a Western woman—dewy-
eyed, slim as a wheat stem, tidily groomed, always smiling
and equally adept at slapping leather—favored a high-
crowned wide-brimmed hat of white felt pushed back to
show off coiffured locks. She wore at all times a sequin
bedecked satin shirt and a divided Dale Evans buckskin
skirt with fringe dripping to butterfly-carved boot tops.
Naturally, while waiting for Roy Rogers to come riding in
from the range, the Western woman carried a braided
horsehair riding crop which she smacked across her palm
as she pondered life.

I knew these things, and I welcomed, even rushed to
purchase, fancy beige and cream boots, a ten gallon white

Stetson, a pink-satin shirt with sequins and pearl snap buttons and a pair of Penney's best blue-denim jeans. (Out West, designer jeans are those not on sale.) Fringed skirts, I discovered, exist in Hollywood or New York, but not in Hiram's Drygoods Store. The store didn't carry braided horsehair riding crops either, but the clerk gave me a free yardstick she said made a pretty good whopping sound when cracked against boots.

Tilting my white Stetson rakishly, I slipped into a pair of dark glasses and commenced to sashay along Main Street. Passersby were stunned. Some even leaned against the nearest building and made snickering noises behind their hands.

Frances went into tasteless hysterics. When she could speak, she informed me I was hurting her eyes. Leading me to the corral, she scooped up handfuls of rich, thick corral dirt and buttered my jeans. Snatching off my sparkling headgear, she threw it to the ground and stirred it among what I hoped were only dirt clumps. The yellow butterflies on my beige boots disappeared as she jerked my pantlegs to the outside.

"There, you look used now. Maybe people won't think you're quite such a dude!" She spat the word out like a bad taste. Confiscating my sunglasses, she yanked my hat down till my eyeballs throbbed. "Out West," she stated, "we shade eyes with hatbrims."

The operative words for Western-dress mode are early drab. Color and variety may be obtained by wearing different colored plaid or flowered shirts, but anything shiny is fair game for ridicule unless you're square dancing. Roy and Dale may wear glossy garments with enough fringe to supply a shoestring factory, but Roy and Dale sing.

The Western hat, a dashing article rarely removed from its owner's cranium, is the primary reason western men look tall. The high crown can conceal lunch, a pointed head or small weapons. As with boots, a cowboy aims to die with his hat on. He wears it in the barnyard, while riding the range, driving the tractor, during a meal (*de rigueur* in restaurants), and while dancing. On those rare occasions when he appears with a naked head (funerals and weddings), the upper third of his brow, where the sun never shines, appears slug white. If he's bald clean back to his collar, he's likely to keep his hat on even when attending funeral or wedding.

No matter how grungy, no headgear is ever thrown away. Check the back porches of any ranch house or bunk house and you will observe a morgue of tattered greasy hats, some mere rags clinging to hatbands. All Western men maintain one or more regulation style cowboy hats "for good."Recent years have seen the advent of baseball-style caps for daily wear largely because they're obtained free from oil, seed and feed companies. As with regular headgear, no caps are ever discarded, but hang like hibernating bats on backporch hooks. Once a year, wives quietly gather up these fossils and incinerate them.

Leather vests have given way to the down-filled polyester, all-weather garments. Leather or down-filled, the vest is removed only in the hottest part of summer. In winter, it is worn as the single warmth item. A jacket is added only when frost-bitten arms start to clank.

Blue jeans have been accepted by Western males as the compleat trouser. Old timers wear them low and slightly baggy. Younger men tend to succumb to painful binding. Tight or loose, to keep his pants in place, the cowboy wears a belt carved with his name or initials and cinched just below his paunch. Wearing a belt at the waistline is a certain sign the individual is a Greenhorn.

The Woolly West will never die as long as there is a cowpoke, tall in the saddle, with hat pulled low, vest over long-sleeved shirt (no genuine cowboy ever wears a short-sleeved shirt—some say it is because his arms go only half way up) and trousers hanging from a belt that appears to C-clamp the upper and lower halves of his body together. A cowboy sets a tone in any gathering. As with royalty, many may aspire, but only the few born-in-the-saddle can claim to be True Cowboys.

EDIFYING WOOLLY WEST EDICTS

When do you see cowpokes, ranch hands or stockmen wearing short-sleeved shirts?
Answer: Never.

• ● •

When do country Western men jog?
Answer: Never. But sometimes they'll run like the dickens to head off or turn back a high-tailing critter.

• ● •

When do Western women wear furs, glamour gowns or makeup?
Answer: Once a year when going to an Uppercrust New Year's party. Or when playing a Soiled Dove in a melodrama.

• ● •

Why don't Western women wear makeup and glamour duds more often?
Answer: They forget.

• ● •

What is accepted dress-for-success garb for country women?

Answer: Coveralls, scabby work shoes, holey hat and shredded gloves. When company comes, take off the coveralls, if you can remember to.

CHAPTER 2

LOCAL SPEECH
(Don't panic, most Westerners speak some English)

Out West, folks talk slower and not necessarily the same English as is spoken in metropolitan areas.

Country men often don't talk at all, but when they do, they repeat each sentence, which helps conversational lag. When two ranchers meet, a typical exchange goes like this:

George: "How's it going?"

Clint: "Oh, could be worse, could be better."

(George and Clint enjoy a pause as each slouches to a hip and commences staring at ground or sky. Spit as needed.)

George: "You git your lambs sold?"

Clint: "Hmmm?"

George: "You git your lambs sold?"

Clint: "Yup."

George: "When'd you ship 'em?"

Clint: "Hmmm?"

George: "When'd you ship 'em?"

Clint: "Last Friday, took a pickup load to market."

George: "Last Friday? Pickup load?"

Clint: "Yup."

George: "Yup."

(George and Clint enjoy another pause. Change slouches to other hips, stare at sky, ground. Spit as needed.

George casually reaches for shirt pocket and extracts snoose.

Clint ditto.

George and Clint each thoughtfully takes a fresh chew, first politely offering some to the other man.)

George: "Git any rain up your way?"

Clint: "What?"

George: "Git any rain up your way?"

And so it goes. Hint to the Greenhorn: Note in the above dialogue that no mention is made of number of lambs sold or price received. It is up to Clint to reveal that information, which he may eventually choose to do especially if they are friends. Asking a rancher acquaintance how many stock he owns or acres he operates is like asking you what your yearly income is in front of company.

EDIFYING WOOLLY WEST EDICTS

To acquire colorful Western speech, never use a plain verb. For example, in any sentence using the verb, "to run", substitute skedaddle, hightail, light out, lope, full-bore flat-out, or, faster than a rooster after a hen.

Heed colloquialisms such as:

"Hang and rattle;" meaning making a big noise or a pest of yourself until noticed.

"Happy as a peach-orchard boar;" meaning you couldn't be happier.

• ● •

What do you say when asked, "How's it going?"

Answer: "Oh, could be worse, could be better."

• ● •

What do you say when you disapprove of someone's action, such as marrying a person of questionable stability?

Answer: "He/she sure drove his/her geese to a poor market."

• ● •

What do you say when a get-together between people of either opposite opinions or excitable personalities or both results in some kind of an uproar?

Answer: "Boy, if that's not a monkey and a parrot situation."

• ● •

What do you say if two people together are strange, an odd match, or slightly off-beat companions?

Answer: "Now, there's a pair to draw to."

• ● •

What do you say when you want to describe the keen cutting ability of a good cowhorse?

Answer: "That horse is so good, he could cut a piss ant away from the sugar bowl."

• ● •

What do you say when an animal or a human is on his last legs and failing fast?

Answer: "That poor old skate hasn't (or ain't got) long to go." In ranch country, ice-skate blades used to be made from the ribs of old horses gone to that Great Pasture in the Sky. Hence, an "old skate" refers to any critter that appears ready to cash in.

• ● •

What do you say when you are completely fed up with an individual and resolve never to have anything more to do with him?

Answer: "Far as I'm concerned, the sun went down on that _____!"

— ● —

CHAPTER 3

PICKUP MYSTIQUE
(Old pickups never die — they're parked in the pasture and started up once a year)

Out West a car is a car, but a pickup is a way of life.

The pickup is **the** means of transportation. No vehicle (with the possible exception of snorting tractors) supplies as much emotional satisfaction as lifting the reins of a prancing 4-wheel-drive pickup. Sometimes, blowing on the wind, a cry can be heard: "Hi Yo , Pickup, Awayyyyyy ."

So deep is the Westerner's attachment to his rubber-

tired horse, the two of them are spoken of in the same
breath. "Joe Smith? Yeah, he's the guy that drives that
blue and white Chevy. Sam Jones? He died last week.
Drove that Ford with the wooden stockrack."

Pickups have a definite herd instinct. In streets and
parking lots, they nuzzle one another, like bulls or wild
horses. Meanwhile their owners banter back and forth
without anyone actually dismounting. Two pickups
meeting on a street will, without guidance, pause, a signal
for their drivers to lop elbows out windows, exchange
remarks and have a chew. When coming across a halted
pair of pickups, do not become testy. Simply call out,
"How's it going?" and drive around.

Any parked pickup is a focal point for a social
phenomenom called, "Pickup Palaver." Men gather like
flies around a tethered pickup and face inward around the
tailgate and sides of the truck, elbows resting on sides or
end panel, hands dangling loosely over the edge. This
stance puts the men in perfect position to stare into the bed
of the truck. Studying truck bottoms facilitates universal,
world and local problem solving. Friendly banter ping-
pongs pleasantly across the truck bed.

Tall men have no problems viewing truck bed interiors. Short ones may have to use the one-armed cling postion, hooking an elbow over a side panel and hanging on. Often the shorties can only eyeball a rear wheel.

Some men prefer not to lean elbows, especially if the weather is bitter. Keeping their hands in their pockets, they use the chest- and stomach-leaning stance, a position that still allows a view into the truck bottom. Always, one of the gathering stands with his **back** propped against the truck, arms folded across his chest, his gaze on the horizon. (In a gaggle of geese, one gander always keeps watch.)

A scientific investigation into whatever lurks in pickups that engages such rapt attention, revealed only bits of straw and hay, tangles of bale strings, rusty shovels, broken iron things, an occasional fence post, empty snoose cans, beer cans and assorted varieties of fecal material.

Pickup palavering tends to be a sexist activity as women are usually too short to obtain a clear view into the truck bed. A person afflicted with shortness needs to be cautious on a cold winter day when chumily joining a palavering group. Opening your mouth to put in two cents worth risks getting your tongue stuck to the cold metal of the side panel. If that happens, pray the pickup owner won't drive off, and commence squeaking as loudly as you can. Finally a Samaritan will notice you trying to eat the truck and maybe pour salt on your stuck tongue. Salt won't make the pickup any tastier, but it will loosen the flesh from the steel. For quite a while, you may favor eating only cool to cold food through a straw.

Pickup palavering does not mean continuous connected comprehensible conversation. One needn't feel snubbed because of long silences. Just keep on a-leaning and a-staring. It takes a heap of staring to generate an utterance. Eventually, a palaverer will scuff a boot on the ground, spit (see chapter on chewing), look at the horizon, adjust his hat and, finally, bring forth a nugget . . . an observation about the excavation out on the highway, an opinion about old man Borkland's new bull or a dire warning about the weather.

Not only do pickups facilitate palavering, they also save shoe leather. Cross into that country called "Out West" and walking becomes a lost art. Even for trips around the block, down to the tavern, or two doors up to the neighbors, the Westerner slips into a pickup as easily as shrugging into his favorite shirt.

Out West, even high-school kids drive pickups, often with floors, sides and ceilings upholstered in dyed sheep pelts. Boys, crammed four to the seat, drive down Main Street, turn right, circle the block, go up Second Street, turn again and blast back up Main.

High-school girls drive their vehicles (usually the family sedan) in the same pattern but in opposite directions. As they pass by each other, the two groups whinny.

Parents become used to seeing only the top half of an offspring through a pickup window. One woman discovered her son had grown three inches the day she caught him in one of his rare appearances outside his truck.

Ranch kids learn to drive right after they learn to walk. Sitting on a stack of boards, they drive to the fields, the mailbox, the corrals, and from the front door to the back door. By the time a ranch kid is old enough to read, he's driven a rut to the school-bus stop at the county road.

Don't panic the first time you see an apparently driverless pickup maneuvering itself along a country road. As the truck draws closer, and you prepare to leap to safety, you'll suddenly note a pair of barely visible eyeballs shining over the dash. The owly orbs belong to a skinny kid obviously guessing where the road is.

During the week, wherever a country lane meets the county road, transportation conveyances awaiting the school bus litter the borrow pits. At day's end, the vehicles pilot themselves, with the help of bug-eyed kids, back to the ranches.

EDIFYING WOOLLY WEST EDICTS

When do you borrow another person's pickup, chain-saw or horse?

Answer: Never, unless he or she originates an offer.

• ● •

When does a pickup owner trade in his old truck on a new one?

Answer: Never. Even when he purchases a new vehicle, he keeps the old one tethered down behind the garage or parked in the old-machinery graveyard. Every so often he goes out and starts it just once more.

If he has kids, they can drive it around the ranch, and if it's still running come fall, they can use it to drive to the school-bus stop.

As part of the family, an old pickup earns a name associated with its color or characteristics, such as "Old Blue," "Old Greenie" or "Old Clank and Rattle."

• ● •

When do country pickup owners repair, paint, fix or renovate their vehicles?

Answer: Never. If the door handle falls off, the rancher uses the other side-door for egress and ingress. If the springs poke through, he throws an old horse blanket over the hole.

• ● •

When do pickup owners use a garage to shelter their trucks?

Answer: Never. In cold weather, they plug in the head-bolt heater to an extension cord strung out a block or so across the barnyard.

CHAPTER 4.

TO CHEW OR NOT TO CHEW...

(Snoose use—how to hold a lip- or cheek-full)

In the Woolly West, a mark of status, particularly for males, is the ability to hold a lipfull of snoose. A messy form of nicotine, snoose refers either to snuff or tobacco, not, as some Greenhorns have been led to believe, a female moose. To "have a chew" or to "take a chew" can refer to a pinch of snuff or a wad of chewing tobacco. Nothing is actually "chewed." The substance is merely held lumpishly inside the face. As with blowing the nose with the fingers, chewing remains an untidy practice, and its joys seem comprehensible mainly to men. Chewers are instantly recognizable because of shirt or hind-pocket stigmata, a condition where the pocket fabric shows a thin circular fungus-like wear ring.

Women chewers are rare, especially if they ever try it. To learn how is not difficult if your stomach is strong.

First, purchase a can of snuff and a packet of chewing tobacco. Snuff, packaged in a flat round can a bit larger than a silver dollar, comes in regular or mint flavor and can be obtained in any Western grocery or bar. The material is so precious it is dated for freshness like a side of meat or a vial of medicine. Break the paper seal by zipping the blade of your pocketknife around the can perimeter. Thump the can lid sharply with your trigger finger. The sharp pain in the digit is a clue to coming enjoyment. Remove the tin lid to reveal an ounce of brown powder that strongly ressembles granulated freeze-dried cow patty. Employ a swirling motion of thumb and two fingers, pinch out a dime-sized portion and pack it in between your lower lip and gum. Immediately, lip skin pooches out as though you have a boil.

Some people prefer packing snuff inside the lip space above the upper teeth. Try both. Either style brings tears to the eyes, induces severe burning of lip and gum and floods the mouth with strange, bitter-brown juice that has a savory flavor reminiscent of mummy wrappings. As your salivary glands activate worse than turned-on fire hoses, you have two choices. Spit or swallow. Decide quickly or chance unsightly drool. Out West a man is known as level headed when snoose juice trails in two even tracks from both sides of his mouth.

Chewing tobacco, also a remarkably nasty substance, is packaged in foil like a nougat bar. Once unwrapped, the tobacco lays there, moist, thready, squashed together like fossilized compost and smells like it. Break off a "plug" from the main hunk and squirrel it inside your cheek cavity, which will make your face appear as if you're trying to eat a billiard ball. Meanwhile, your mouth will fill with brown juice. Hold your breath, and try not to swallow. (This may be an unnecessary instruction.) Enjoy the violent stinging as brown liquid surges up your sinuses.

Scientifically collected data on chewing and chewers reveals that a chewer's life focuses on where to spit, when to spit and what in or at. Chewers fall into recognizable spitting types. There is the hold-it-till-the-last-possible-second spitter. A chain chewer, he has to have some snoose in his face all of his waking hours. With lower lip jutted like a pelican's beak, he speaks without moving his lower jaw. When the snoose juice fills his face to overflowing, he becomes desperate and lets go in potted plants, under the edge of anybody's carpet, in a room corner, behind a radiator, in a coffee cup . . . spitters have no shame. They avoid looking anyone in the eye, believing that without eye contact, no one notices what they're doing. They shyly spit in gutters, doorways, or in personal coffee-can spittoons. Once a greenhorn mistakenly put a charitable dime in a man's can.

Sharp shooting spot-spitters become so expert, they often hire out as hit men during grasshopper plagues. On Saturday nights when the wind isn't blowing, contests are held to determine the "fastest spit in the West."

Pickup palaverers who congregate to stare into pickup bottoms, develop an easy rhythm of staring and spitting. Resting forearms on a truck's panel sides, the chewer angles the lower half of his body a foot away. Bowing his head as if praying, he bombs the dust directly between his feet. With this method a spitter avoids splattering his neighbor or having to turn out into the wind.

Right after mail delivery at the post office, groups of men loiter about, chatting and spitting. Each speaker punctuates each remark with a friendly "pa-tooie!" into the gutter. It is best to stand on the upwind side of fast talkers.

At the entrance of any building frequented by snoose users, you will note brown globs polka-dotting the ground. (Geese cause similar mottled texturing on doorsteps.) It is considered gentlemanly to voluntarily de-snoose before entering a public eating place or a church. Stepping to the curb, the chewer rids his wad with a quick sagital bend and snap of the head. To avoid slovenly soil, amateur chewers should practice the sideways bend, the headsnap and the rid-the-wad spit until they achieve one smooth motion. If trapped with no place to spit, a gentleman simply swallows. Many men claim the liqueur rids the body of worms and cures hemorrhoids. No one has ever disproved the claim.

In moving vehicles, chewers roll down a convenient window and fire at the landscape. At no time is it wise to sit in the back seat of any conveyance, moving or not, if the windows are open. Snoose tracks on the inside of a car window indicate an absent minded, rude or lousy-shot spitter. When driving behind a pickup whose driver is a known chewer, keep the wipers going, particularly if the day is windy.

To snoose or not to snoose . . . that is the question. Those who can withstand the slings and arrows of disgust, not to mention the slobber and stain of snoose juice, will find the Woolly West a chewer's heaven.

EDIFYING WOOLLY WEST EDICTS

Under what circumstances will snoose users give up the habit?

Answer: Death. Maybe.

• ● •

At what age do snoose users pick up the habit?

Answer: Age 12 for the average Western kid, eight years old for the precocious, and 16 for late bloomers and sissies.

• ● •

Does a snoose chewer clean up his own spittoons?

Answer: Not if he's married to an easily intimidated or a Greenhorn woman.

• ● •

How does an easily intimidated or super-tidy woman refrain from having to clean up yucky snoose-spoiled containers?

Answer: a) Throw the spittoons in the creek.
        b) Permanently close the kitchen to snoose users.
        c) Close the bedroom door from your side until you come to an agreement.
        d) All of the above.

PART II

WOOLLY WEST CUSTOMS

TIPS ON HOW TO FIT IN

CHAPTER 5

GOING TO TOWN
*(Hints on where to find practically everybody
— somewhere around town)*

Woolly-West town business districts comprise no more than two or three blocks on Main Street with a sprinkling of enterprises on side streets. Going to town is a Significant Social Event.

Sociability starts, for rural dwellers, from the moment the pickup is fired up and pointed townward. Encounters with cars or trucks enroute require particular responses and specific gestures. Greeting an approaching conveyance driven by an acquaintance, calls for lifting the hand, palm out, fingers spread, accompanied by a wave, smile and nod. The degree of enthusiasm depends on how well you know the other party, but not how well you like them.

To an unknown driver whose face (or truck) seems familiar, keep hands gripped on the steering wheel, but lift four fingers straight up. As you pass, flutter fingers. The totally unknown driver piloting a conveyance bearing home-county license plates warrants sticking up one index finger—no finger flutter.

Regardless of driver acquaintanceship, any stock-truck or tractor receives a one- to four-finger flutter. Drivers of out-of-state transportation receive a penetrating gaze but no wave, flutter or nod.

Arriving in town, rural vehicles tether themselves without guidance in front of the post office. It is unwise to remain parked at the P.O. for longer than the duration of mail pickup. Trucks and cars left longer than ten minutes are viewed as permanent fixtures against which town philosophers will lean and drape themselves. Back away suddenly and you chance inflicting bodily injury on a pontificating draper.

Twice a week, in the country, a mail person slogs through rain or hail or heat of day to deliver messages to ranch and farm. Mail is shoved into metal boxes shaped like mini quonset huts perched on a post a minimum of half-a-muddy-mile from your house. In nasty weather it is friendly, even life saving, to leave something homebaked in the mailbox. On severely inclement winter days, leave an invitation in the box to come to the house for hot coffee and cookies. Besides being a humane gesture, it establishes a friendly ambience which may be important the day you need desperately to get to town, and all your own transportation is broke down, including your horse. Accepting and eating gifts along the mail route explains why no one ever sees a skinny mail carrier.

Town dwellers save on baking and coffee brewing because mail in town must be personally fetched. Daily, someone of every household strolls to the post office. Or they ride bicycles. Robust senior folks ride three wheelers while less athletic oldsters take a daily constitutional walk.

Entering, lingering or leaving the P.O. premises requires wearing a post-office smile. No toothy beam. A simple, pleasant tilt of lip corners will suffice. For small towners, exchanging medical opinions and health-status updates is crucial, but it is important to discuss only the highlights while inside the building. Avoid extended indoor consultations as they tend to bottleneck doorways which could endanger someone's already precarious health. Persons engaged in in-depth conversations must move to the bench outside or down the street to the drug store.

Next stop is the grocery store. In addition to selling

meats and vegetables, a small town grocery also acts as a communication center.

Shopping carts cruising grocery aisles behave similarly to pickups in the streets. When one cart meets another, it pauses while its driver gabs. Such talk is called "cart confab." Cart confabs reveal the latest love and/or sex scandals, whose son got into trouble, whose daughter is pregnant, who poached a deer, who passed on and when the funeral will take place. Lean on a shopping cart long enough and you can find out whatever you missed hearing at the post office.

Grocery aisles clogged with carts whose drivers are busy confabulating might frustrate the newcomer. But relax. Avoid elevated blood pressure. Do not become testy. Pause with your own cart and join in. You may possess that absolutely vital missing piece of information. Especially if the subject is you.

EDIFYING WOOLLY WEST EDICTS

How often do waitpersons refill your coffee cup in Western restaurants?

Answer: Every three seconds.

• ● •

Out West, where do you go for the best, most generous plain meal?

Answer: To the restaurant next to the Stockyards.

• ● •

What does the Stockyard restaurant serve?

Answer: Breakfast: Sausage-gravy and biscuits; sausage-gravy, biscuits and eggs, or sausage-gravy, biscuits, eggs and steak.

Dinner: (sometimes referred to as Lunch by Greenhorns) Meat, potatoes, gravy, salad, vegetable, homemade rolls and rhubarb pie.

Supper: (sometimes referred to as Dinner by Greenhorns) Meat, potatoes, gravy, salad, vegetable, homemade rolls and rhubarb pie with ice cream.

CHAPTER 6

COFFEE HOUR . . . AFTER HOUR . . . AFTER HOUR
(Westerners have strong kidneys)

Out West, social groups meeting for coffee are stratified according to the availability of unoccupied time, not economic level or occupation. At ten a.m., it is against the law for anyone to become ill, spring a leak, commit a crime or need uplifting, since the Doc, the plumber, the Sheriff and the Reverend are having coffee at the Oxbow Restaurant. In an emergency, persons in dire need can join the coffee klatchers to discuss their individual problems, but they can't expect action until after 10:15. One pregnant woman stopped by the Oxbow to tell Doc she believed she was going into labor. Doc invited her to sit down and rest a moment. While she was quite happy to join the group, she rested a tad too long. The town still talks about the time Doc delivered a baby in the private dining room of the Oxbow. Since then, Doc has never invited a pregnant woman to sit down.

Senior curmudgeons, known as the Superannuated Irregulars, coffee at the bakery where they shove together two or three tables, order gooey sweets with their caffeine and chew over issues and scandals, some recent and some from 35 to 60 years ago. This makes for an interesting historical review as past and present scandals sometimes involve the same people.

Across from the bakery, the drugstore serves as headquarters for business people and storekeepers from up and down Main Street. It's best to avoid shopping in the clothing stores or requesting information at the Court House or expecting service from City Hall between 10 and 10:15, as the personnel have all gone to coffee. However, it is all right to join them during their break and chat while waiting. When you do that though, it's best to bring your own rolls and share with everyone.

EDIFYING WOOLLY WEST EDICTS

Out West, when can medical emergencies occur?
Answer: Anytime except Doc's day off, especially if it's a messy emergency.

•●•

To locate anybody in a small town, what do you do?

Answer: a) Stand in the post office at ten a.m. on the day
the local paper is published and delivered to
the P.O. boxes.

b) Drive up and down Main Street till you spot
the person's car.

• ● •

What do you do when you spy a stranger on the street?

Answer: Engage the person in conversation and ask if he
or she is related to the Svensons. If the person says no, en-
courage him or her to reveal ethnic orgins and local ties.
Once you elicit a faintly recognizable name, clever fishing
can draw forth the stranger's entire personal history while
revealing none of your own.

• ● •

How do you avoid having to stop and chat while in a small-
town grocery if you're in a terrible rush?

Answer: You don't. You must drive to the store in the next
town, but wear dark glasses and a different hairdo.

• ● •

How do you find an address in a small town?

Answer: a) Never by street number. The house is always referred to by the name of the first owners some fifty or sixty years ago.

b) It is further described by the color it was first painted sixty years ago, but may have no bearing on the present hue.

c) Location is finally pinned down by mentioning the name of the person living across the street or down the block or next to the church.

CHAPTER 7

HOW TO UNDERSTAND US HICKS
(Out West everybody wears patched pants)

The Greenhorn arriving at his chosen Western Paradise, often suffers from a glowing desire to recreate it in his own image. He finds it a perfect haven needing only a few small changes to make it more like the world he just hurried to leave. A burning fervor to improve Paradise drives some newcomers to attempt to update, upgrade, uplift, upeducate local yokels so that they will become appreciators of the arts, theater, music, assorted culture and, of course, lovers of nature as indeed, all Greenhorns know themselves to be.

While it is possible the newcomers' motives stem from a lofty position of well-bred culture, sophistication and a generous yearning to share their refinement, the locals may be hard to convince. Pointing out that the big Metropolis back East has free museums, plentiful bakeries, elegant shops and culture that drips down the sides of every mile-high edifice will fail to impress the provincials. It is the wise Greenhorn who realizes that the locals not only are not grateful for the information, but they invariably snicker at efforts to lift them from the bog of hickdomry. Out West there's a slogan, "Say what you want, but don't push!" which sometimes leaves the Greenhorn with nothing to talk about.

Trying to find a particular level of society with which to identify can also be difficult for the newcomer used to specific and precise social strata. Out West, the social upper and undercrust meld together to a disconcerting degree for those unused to rubbing elbows with the hoi-polloi. The local 400 consists of only three families, one of whom is wintering in Tahiti, and the other two of whom aren't speaking. Alas, it can be lonely at the top.

To be an uppercrust member, your family must have owned land for at least three generations back, which is why the top crust is so thin. To become speedily accepted on the ordinary level, join every organization from Garden Club to Horseshoe Pitching. Attend every community function from Grade School Art Exhibit to the 4-H Fair. Become a member of the church denomination of your choice.

However, joining organizations and attending community functions are not required in a Woolly West town. Should you indicate a desire to be left alone, Westerners will respect your wishes and leave you alone . . . forever.

To view local people as quaint, charming and possibly ignorant bumpkins who talk loudly, use bad grammer and lean on shovels, is a mistake. It could be years or perhaps forever before you discover many of the shovel-leaners graduated from Yale, Harvard or Radcliffe. Some of the loud-talking bumpkins own their own airplanes and may fly to Seattle or Denver for a meal when the whim strikes. Others may be on a first name basis with Heads of State, or be nuclear experts or are best-selling authors and playwrights. It's hard to draw conclusions about a shovel-leaner's pedigree at first glance. By the time you sort out the leaner's social levels, you will have provided pickup palaverers with a whole truckload of laughs.

EDIFYING WOOLLY WEST EDICTS

Whom do you invite to a Western small-town or country wedding?

Answer: Anyone you want.

•●•

Whom do you invite to a Western small-town wedding reception and/or dance?

Answer: Absolutely everyone.

•●•

Where is a Western small-town wedding reception held?

Answer: The church basement if large enough, otherwise, the Moose Hall.

•●•

How do you invite everyone to a wedding dance or reception?

Answer: Put an ad in the local paper announcing the event. Those who want to come, will, and none of the rest of the community will feel snubbed at not receiving a personal invitation.

• ● •

How and when do you offer helpful advice to Westerners?

Answer: Never. It is considered a rude intrusion and none of your business to offer unsolicited comments or advice, no matter how apt or beneficial to a person engaged in any task whatsoever.

• ● •

As a Greenhorn eager to learn, when **can** you ask questions?

Answer: Never while the Western he or she is engaged in doing outside chores or inside chores. It is considered rude to fire questions while someone is busy. Wait till later over coffee. Then ask, but speak slowly.

• ● •

When will a Western small-town or rural person volunteer comments or advice on something you are doing?

Answer: Never, unless you make a specific request. You will then receive a nonchalant third-person directive, such as, "Well, they say maybe a person could do, try, consider . . ." followed by the instruction. If you want continuing enlightenment, don't argue and don't expect the advice to be repeated.

• ● •

In your own home, when do you serve coffee to visitors?
Answer: Everytime.

• ● •

What do you do when people drop by to visit, and they haven't been invited?
Answer: Serve them coffee.

• ● •

What do you do when people drop by to visit, and you really can't stand them?
Answer: Serve coffee.

• ● •

When do you offer cake, pie, or cookies to go with the coffee?
Answer: Everytime.

• ● •

What is the average length of a telephone call Out West?
Answer: Seven minutes. Five minutes to discuss heat, cold, rain, when school starts this year, how's the garden growing and what to do for a sinus condition. Two minutes to mention the reason you've phoned: "Say, what I called about is . . ."

CHAPTER 8

MATT DILLON, FESTUS, MISS KITTY AND THE POSSE
(No matter what the problem — call the Sheriff)

In the Woolly West, law officers no longer ride horses on duty, but they still carry guns, drink coffee and keep eagle eyes on the lookout for bad guys.

Some towns are so little, they require only a town constable, a man whose primary duty is to make sure the bars close up at the correct hour, rattle doorknobs of business places in case somebody forgot to lock up, and chase home the kids caught out after curfew.

Many towns have only a County Sheriff, an Undersheriff, half a dozen Deputies, a Detective (a deputy with a merit badge) and a police dog. The police dog is 100 pounds of Shepherd who, on command, attacks nefarious culprits, sniffs out dope, intimidates malcontents and can be seen licking babies and playing fetch-the-stick with neighborhood children.

If and when additional law enforcement personnel may be needed, the Sheriff's Posse is called out. A posse is a collection of private citizens, usually male, who volunteer to help out whenever there's a Saturday night dance, during the Rodeo weekend, during the hometown ballgames, and the Fourth of July celebrations.

You may have occasion to call the Sheriff:

. . . to report a neighbor's noisy dog is keeping you awake.

. . . to report you've lost your wallet, your dog, your kid.

. . . if you or someone you know imbibes too much alcoholic refreshment and shouldn't be driving. A Deputy will haul home your carcass or give you a night's lodging in the jail, a cement lined apartment with no windows, no TV, and no lid on the toilet. It does, however, have a night light.

. . . if you are being kept awake by noisy parties, noisy drag races, noisy kids in the park after curfew.

. . . if you are approached by weird persons selling anything door-to-door.

. . . if you are approached by weird persons selling trinkets and soliciting money for an odd cause you've never heard of.

. . . if somebody's cows or sheep are out on the public highway.

. . . if somebody's cows or sheep are in your yard.

Besides catching villains and helping the weak, the unfortunate and the mildly defective, the Sheriff's Deputies also meet the victorious high-school ballteam's bus a mile out of town and give them a rousing, siren-blowing, lights-flashing welcome-home escort.

Sheriff's Deputies are also called upon to inspect brands on livestock. This means they must go to a ranch and stare at burn marks on the sides of assorted livestock. This is what gives the Western lawman that steely-eyed squint.

EDIFYING WOOLLY WEST EDICTS

How do Sheriffs and Deputies spell hello and goodbye?
Answer: Ten-four.

• ● •

When driving in a small town, are you required to stop at corners?
Answer: Only if you're under 70.

• ● •

In small towns Out West, do elderly ladies drive?
Answer: Absolutely. Should you notice an aged Cadillac, Buick, Pontiac or '46 GMC pickup rolling along the street apparently driverless except for a bit of gray fluff barely

visible over the top of the dash—relax. It's only Mrs. Heckerson on her way to the grocery store.

• ● •

How do you identify a stray dog and locate its owner?

Answer: Ask any six-year-old kid. He/she will know the canine's name and where it lives. The kid won't, however, know the dog-owner's name, but can lead you to the proper residence. It's up to you to knock on the door.

— ● —

CHAPTER 9

BARN-YARD SHISH-KE-BAB
(Farmer Fondue)

During my first summer in my newly adopted community, I agreed to help my friend, Frances, manage an outdoor summer function called, Farm/City Appreciation Day. On F/C Day, farmers and ranchers barbecue donated beef and mutton, and town folks down it with relish.

In the tiny uptown park, a narrow landscaped space between two buildings, tables and benches circled an iron pot big enough to boil a missionary. The kettle was suspended by a log chain from a tepee-pole arrangement. Beneath the pot, a leaping fire kept ten gallons of hog fat bubbling, while the Chamber of Commerce Chief stirred the brew with a borrowed canoe paddle.

On a table, large metal trays held mounds of peeled sliced potatoes.Similar trays held raw, bleeding, bite-sized meat chunks. A brand new pitchfork, its tines gleaming wickedly, lay beside the meat.

Frances busily assigned duties. A potato-dipper person scooped sliced potatoes into a strainer large enough to seine ocean fish, then immersed the spuds into boiling fat. It was a little like dipping sheep in a vat of tick solution. Thick, elbow-length kitchen mitts protected the potato dipper from searing hot grease.

Frances assigned two persons the task of overseeing mustard, ketchup, soda-pop and napkin dispensing. Then she picked up the shiny pitchfork and came at me. Nervously I backed away. "Your job," she said, "is to load the shish onto the fork."

Ignoring the squeamish flutter in my middle, I picked up a gob of slippery, diced beef or mutton—there were no labels. Because the fork stood taller than my head, I had to lift a piece of meat high and attempt to impale it downward onto a tine. Meat juice trickled down my arm and dripped off my elbow making me attractive to the Sheriff's dog who sat, tongue lolling, guarding something.

Once the fork tines were loaded, I staggered to the cauldron and fondued. The first few times, the heavy load nearly pole-vaulted me into the bubbling fat which taught me to skewer fewer at a time. Allowing the meat a moment to brown nicely, I then lifted it from the lard bath, jousted through the crowd to a large roasting pan where a helpful shish-scraper knocked the shish off the tines. Fork cleared, I returned to skewer some more. I felt a little like Nanook of the North cooking up a catch of whale blubber.

The tiny park could barely accommodate tables, benches, cauldron and people, but it really became congested when 23 members of the high-school band, with instruments, joined the festivities. Frances said they had come to provide background music.

"Where?" I asked. "We're packed in like sardines now."

The kids solved the space problem by bunching in a corner on top of petunias freshly planted by the garden-club ladies. On a count of three, they struck up a lively version of "The Gang's All Here." As I maneuvered past them, the trombonist slide-tromboned right into my loaded pitchfork. Eight pieces of meat jumped off my fork, and the Sheriff's dog caught seven before they hit the ground.

Meanwhile, groups of elderly folks, seated on benches around serving tables, happily partook of free shish, spuds and coffee. When the noon whistle blew, hungry business lunchers squeezed into the fray. Some retired sheepherders filled their plates six or seven times, and a passing collie challenged the Sheriff's canine over a dropped hunk of meat. The collie was arrested. Little kids tore around throwing pop at one another. Frances bustled here and there making sure sliced spuds got deep-dunked and shish-ke-bab got shished.

On one of her sashays past me, she urged, "Hurry up with the meat. People are waiting."

I skewered as fast as I could, but my fork loading fell behind, especially as the wind started blowing just short of hurricane strength. Trying to stick gobs of meat on a tall pitchfork in the teeth of a 40-knot gale required more strength than I could muster. Necessity encouraged me to develop an alternate meat-loading method.

Turning my back to the wind, I slanted the fork handle at an angle from my body so that the tines rested against my bosom. Caution: turn the tines outward from your person during fork loading or chance inadvertent acupuncture. The new method lent greater stability and speed to the loading procedure but ruined my shirt front.

By three o'clock we Farm/City Appreciator Personnel had fed up half a beef, three sheep and heaven only knows how many potatoes. Though my weary arms threatened to fall off, I had fondued on in spite of wind, blaring trombones, three blisters and the repulsive mess on my hands. Pride-of-pitchfork prowess bloomed in my soiled bosom when one elderly codger winked at me, smacked his lips and croaked, "You got a right good do on that there mutton, girl. . ."

In the Woolly West, praise and pretty words are everywhere.

EDIFYING WOOLLY WEST EDICTS

To which community functions is one expected to bring a hot dish?

Answer: All of them.

• ● •

Where can you go to dance to a comb, jug, spoons and a couple of fiddles?

Answer: The Senior Citizen Center.

• ● •

If you happen to be a member, especially a female member, of a family that arrived by wagon train with the first settlers, how are you introduced?

Answer: Always as, "Joe Doakes' oldest girl," no matter how old you are or whether or not Joe died some years back.

PART III

WOOLLY WEST GOODS AND SERVICES

DON'T BURN DOWN THAT OUTHOUSE

CHAPTER 10

HOW TO BEHAVE WHEN PATRONIZING LOCAL MERCHANTS AND SHOPKEEPERS

(How to mosey while shopping)

Greenhorns new to the West sometimes make the mistake of believing that store personnel, shopkeepers, clerks and waitpersons are there to serve. This error may cause you some emotional turmoil.

One of the confusing customs is that most businesses in small towns, except for the grocery and the post office, close at noon so that personnel can go home for dinner. Out West, dinner is at noon. The evening meal is called supper.

Since you can't find anything open, you may as well drop in at one of the local restaurants that are open during mealtimes, except on the first day of hunting or fishing season. But that's okay because there's nobody left in town anyway, including the Sheriff.

Restaurants in Western small towns frequently cater to what they feel is your best interest despite your preference. If you're hesitant about what to order, the waitperson will bring you something she believes you should have such as split-pea soup even if you hate split-pea soup. The cook and owner of the establishment (the individual waiting on you) will insist **her** soup is perfectly splendid, and that you will love it. She is right. From then

on you are an addict of split-pea soup . . . hers anyway. It
is wise to show due respect for whomever is serving you.
She or he may be the minister's wife or the minister, the
Mayor's mother or father, or own the dwelling you live in.

Printed restaurant menus are not always a reliable
guide to the fare, nor does an ostentatious exterior facade
on the building have a bearing on food quality. Sometimes
the sleaziest of taverns serve meals so sumptuous, one meal
can support life for a week.

Tiny roadside eateries often operated by a cheery
woman named Mary Lou, who "just loves to cook," can
leave you staggering from overeating.

When traveling in byways Out West, don't overlook
the small tavern-restaurant, usually one of two businesses
in a town, the other being a gas station. Westerners have
a habit of craving seafood. To satisfy that craving, the
tavern owner periodically will have a dozen varieties of
seafood shipped in by airfreight. Then he throws a huge
feed and invites the community to partake of 12 kinds of
seafood, including squid, oysters on the half shell cooked
to perfection, 11 kinds of salad, three kinds of potatoes,
homemade rolls and jellies, condiments and pickles. The
meal begins, of course, with an enormous bowl of clam
chowder made with real cream. Should you stumble onto
one of these repasts, take advantage and belly up. For
$8.95 you can afford to blow your diet.

In general-merchandise stores and shops, do not
become impatient when the clerk continues a comfortable
conversation with another person obviously not there making a purchase. Refrain from tapping impatiently on
counters. Take your time, walk around some, look at objects and eventually mosey over near the confabulators and
join in. Discuss the weather, the crops, the kids, the school
picnic and when hunting season will open. At an oppor-
tune break in the discussion, mention what it was you had

in mind to buy. At first, you'll find it difficult and perhaps awkward trying to guess just when to speak up. Too soon and you'll be ignored. Too late and someone else will have captured the clerk's attention, and you'll have to wait through another rundown of weather, crops and kids.

At lumberyards, grain elevators and feed stores where the merchandise is heavy, don't just stand there. Help. Lift that board and tote that bale to the pickup. While the employee will gladly load for you, it's considered bad form Out West to stand back and watch another person do all the work. If your leg is broken, your arms will still work, so don't hang back.

At the grain elevator, never drive up to the door and honk for service. To do so will earn you a negative reputation you may never live down. Palaverers around pickups will spit and shake their heads sadly as they share the mournful story of the greenhorn who sits and honks. Correct procedure is to get out of your vehicle, saunter into the office and lean on the counter. Josh and banter with the personnel, then mention your wants. If you can't lift the 100-pound sack of oats you've ordered, you're still required to accompany the employee while he slings the sack onto his shoulder and lugs it to the car or truck. Your responsibility is to make friendly remarks all the while.

Should you require a load of loose grain to be funneled into your truckbed, remember you must crawl up and help stomp it down evenly. This means doing a sort of jig to make sure the grain gets deposited in the corners instead of remaining a tall cone in the center of the truck bed. While dancing your jig, it's good form to carry on a friendly conversation with the also-jigging elevator employee.

EDIFYING WOOLLY WEST EDICTS

Where do you find a dolly to use hauling home the new appliance you bought from one of the two appliance stores in town?

Answer: From the other appliance store.

• ● •

Do small town mercantiles and grocery stores Out West have delivery service?

Answer: Absolutely. The store owner will drop off the item on his way home after work. Or he will put it in your car parked downtown and naturally never locked. Or he will leave it at the drugstore with your name on the package.

• ● •

In a small town Out West, what do you do if you become ill?

Answer: Put on a big pot of coffee because an hour after you get your prescription from the drugstore, five people will phone sympathy and two will fetch you a hot dish.

— ● —

CHAPTER 11

RUMMAGE SALES

*(Where recycling is a way of life, a hobby and
a passion)*

Small-town rummage sales are social and cultural events where both the minister's wife and the town's leading-businessman's spouse buy fall wardrobes.

Church congregations try to throw away only the loveliest things. Because lovely rummage is a matter of pride among Christians, different denominations compete to donate the best possible trash items. Sometimes an article, brand new, is purchased at a sale, donated to another sale, purchased again and re-donated.

Competition is so keen that spotters attend rival rummages to check on pricing and variety. Last year, Ursula Pipsworthing of the Episcopal persuasion, contributed three sets of lined, embossed drapes, sold them for $3 a pair, and the Congregationalists grew green with unholy envy. The next week, at **their** rummage sale, 14 pairs of drapes were donated by the faithful and sold for only $2.50 a pair. For months, six Congregational homes went drapeless. There would have been more naked windows, but two Congregational ladies had bought drapes from the Episcopal sale.

Getting rummage ready to merchandise is done with volunteer labor, especially newcomer volunteers. All year long, church members collect clothing, unwanted gifts and oddments too fine to throw away but too useless to keep. Before sale day, women toting armloads of cast-off treasures converge on the house of worship. Then volunteers beaver among the multitudinous containers, unpacking, sorting and pricing. The process is akin to excavating an archeological discovery. Workers exhume tarnished jewelry, shards of pottery, funny beads, and, once, the mumified remains of an unwitting church mouse.

A privilege alloted to all rummage workers is the right to preview and purchase choice donations. Sadly, mining these treasures induces an atmosphere of snatch-and-grab greed, almost overwhelming the kindly spirit of Christian fellowship.

Experienced rummage sorters like Thelma Thiddle utilize the quick-hand, bland-smile combination in pursuit of coveted items. Casual as a grazing cow, Thelma sidles near a box being unpacked by Mrs. Pipsworthing. Bland smile pasted across her lips, Thelma filches a really nice, hardly worn leather purse out of Mrs. Pipsworthing's box.

It's wise to remain alert for claim jumpers. Allowing attention to be diverted may cost you that darling kitchen clock shaped like a pair of crossed corncobs. Exercise strict control over your reactions and, above all, avoid physical violence. Keep in mind that untoward emotional display tends to alienate fellow Christians.

As you dig, refrain from snide comments regarding exhumed items. When viewing a purple-and-green-striped floor-length garment with gold butterfly wings, control your urge to laugh. Crass remarks such as, "Whoever had the lack of taste to wear a ridiculous thing like this?" will draw poisonous looks from the garment's former owner, always the woman standing next to you.

Don't miss acquiring the box of cracked, down-at-the-heels cowboy boots. Once they're filled with buckshot, shellacked all over, and nailed to a board, a pair of crumbly, ordorous scabby boots become charming conversation-piece bookends. Many a guest will want to know where you got them. Also garner that old weathered wooden stirrup. With a hole drilled in it and a pipe stuck through, the stirrup can be reborn as a totally clever lamp base. After a few years, you can donate both the bookends and the lamp to the rummage sale of your choice.

After two days of sorting and pricing, you and the other volunteers pridefully view the laden tables, the sorted piles, the arranged knick-knacks. At nine o'clock on sale day, the doors fly open and hordes of passionate women boil inside, the whites of their eyes flashing as each one feverishly attempts to be first to spot the best treasures.

Watch out for gray-haired bargain hunters who form a flying wedge, mowing down obstacles in their path. Step aside to avoid being run down by a young woman who, balancing an infant on one hip, lopes over to an ancient upright piano (all churches have ancient upright pianos). Picketed along the piano's top, blank-faced styrofoam heads stare like alien beings from under an assortment of wigs. When the woman slips a curly blonde number over her dark hair, the baby on her hip bursts into screams.

In the curtain corner, excited women burrow among the piles, unfolding panels full length across the traffic lane. A small child bashes into a stretched out drape and ka-booms like a rubber ball, smack against the backs of its mother's knees. She collapses to her prayer bones and stays there, knee-walking along as she riffles through sweaters heaped on a bench under the table.

Knick-knack bargain hunters usually head straight for the hard rummage and scoop up armloads of chipped flower pots, discarded record holders, plastic toys, dented cooking pots, odd pieces of dishware, ceramic gew-gaws, mystery gadgets and all but one of six bun warmers.

Other women, arms flailing faster than a nervous octopus, mulligan stew the stacked clothing you've worked so hard to fold and arrange. After awhile, special rummage-selection techniques employed by individual shoppers become apparent. One tall woman, convinced the best articles are on the bottom, reaches a long arm across and flops over a pile, like dumping a turtle on its back. Next to her, a short woman, unable to employ the reach across and flop method, backs away a step, executes a little hippity-hop and dives in, burrowing completely under the heap. She surfaces on the other side waving a pair of thermal underdrawers.

A grandmotherly woman with blue marcelled hair tidily tucked inside a hairnet covetously eyes an item near the top of a high mound. Snatching a rickety wooden stool off the hard-rummage table, Granny parks it next to the clothing mountain, makes a flying-squirrel leap to the top of the heap, snares her prize and skiis down the opposite slope.

In the footwear department, two women are trying on a pair of red pumps. The first lady has on the left pump and the other lady is wearing the right one. Each woman discovers **her** pump fits perfectly. Discussion ensues. Who will leave with two shoes? Rummage-shopping rules say that if you have your hand on an item, it's yours till you lift your hand. Easily intimidated persons with weak grasps have no place at a rummage sale.

By four o'clock, the piles are reduced to stirred rubble, which is then marked down to ten cents an item, bringing on a slight flurry of traffic. At five, leftovers become free to anyone willing to haul them away. After that, the remainder is shoveled into boxes. As a newcomer, you will be privileged to volunteer to help cart the leftovers to the State Institution for the Mentally Confused and Oddly Clothed.

EDIFYING WOOLLY WEST EDICTS

What do you do with all the trash, treasure and artifacts you acquire at yard sales, auctions, rummage sales and bazaars?

Answer: Hold your own yard, garage or auction sale. This finances your next-year's sale-buying habit.

• ● •

When you have a yard sale, how do you prevent people coming early, sometimes getting you out of bed?

Answer: Close and lock doors and windows. Draw the blinds, don't answer phone or door till the appointed sale hour.

• ● •

What time should you go to a yard sale advertised to begin at 9 a.m.?

Answer: 7 a.m.

• ● •

How do you insure getting the very best bargains ahead of everyone else at a rummage sale?

Answer: a) Join five churches and volunteer to help sort rummage.

b) Even before sorting, someone has to gather. Offer your services and car as a rummage collector. Finally, offer your basement or garage as a storage center previous to the sale.

CHAPTER 12

HIGH ON THE HOG
(Bacon does not grow on trees!)

Steaks and chops in the Woolly West do not always appear neatly wrapped in plastic on supermarket styrofoam trays. My first lesson in on-the-hoof, claw or web meat selection occurred the day Frances invited me to help her haul a live hog to the meat-processing plant.

It was a lovely spring day, and I dressed in my Western best—new jeans, snap button shirt and pointy-toed boots. Frances drove the pickup outfitted with a stockrack (a steel cage designed to keep four-footed food from wandering).

At the pork farm, she deftly backed the pickup against the loading chute. Inside the hog corral, an enclosure the size of a motel lobby, a crowd of porkers lolled about. Some were soaking their hoggie hides in a mud jacuzzi. Others snoozed in the shade. Still others snacked grain from individual serving troughs daisy-petaled around a huge, metal, drum-shaped container the size of a taco stand.

Personal selection of on-the-hoof meat is a Western rule. Picking your own meat absolves the livestock grower from responsibility should you select a spavinned, no account, razor backed, pitiful excuse of an animal. Out West, no one would ever be so rude as to point out your stupidity.

Following Frances' lead, I scaled the corral fence and sat down on the top rail. Below me, the hog farmer waved a welcome, and 30 or 40 hogs, roused from their beauty naps, grunted, snorted and loped over to investigate. I drew up my feet.

"Come on," said Frances as she jumped down amongst the rabble.

"You want me in there?" Horrified, I gazed into 40 pairs of little piggy eyes, glittering with possibly homicidal lust. Courage, I told myself, and slid off the top rail. My new Tony Lama boots sank into something offal up to the ankles. Immediately, what seemed like 500 curious hogs closed in. Lordy, I hoped these weren't killer pigs. Frances seemed unconcerned so I remained where I was. I had to. My feet were mired in mud the consistency of igneous gorp.

"HERD 'EM OVER THIS WAY," yelled the pork farmer.

Herd 'em? How was I supposed to do that? Windmilling my arms, I howled, "SHOO, PIGGY, SHOO!"

Startled pigs, some of whom were snuffling muddy snouts on my pants legs, snorted, grunted, squealed and ran off in all directions. Frances (who had cleverly worn four-buckle overshoes and scabby clothing) plopped through the mire in an easterly tack to head them off at the pass. The pig farmer dashed westerly. With great effort, I unplugged my feet from the bog and took two squishy steps before the undertow got me. I splatted to my knees. To keep from burying my face, I quickly straight-armed and sank in to my elbows, whereupon a friendly hog tenderly played kissy face. "Yick!" Two other porkers circled to my rear, muttering sympathy. When they began nuzzling, I rose with admirable alacrity.

By this time, Frances and the farmer had managed to herd eight or ten hogs into a small holding pen.

With a thoop and a thup, I extricated my feet from the gorp, slogged over and crawled into the pen with the pork farmer, Frances and ten hogs.

Eyeing the swine selection, Frances seemed to think there were differences among them. I stared, pretending I knew what I was doing. Finally, Frances said, "That one," indicating the chubby, spotted pig engaged in munching my leg. Reaching down, I scratched its back. Porky grunted with pleasure and stretched out, inviting more.

"Friendly critter," I said, trying to sound Western.

The hog farmer said nothing. He simply picked up an old piece of board and began edging the hog into the loading-chute alleyway, a long, board-sided corridor leading onward for about ten yards before sloping up to meet the backend of the pickup. Frances scooted up the chute ahead of the pig. "I'll lift the gate on the stockrack," she called. "You bring the hog."

I mistakenly thought she was talking to the pork farmer, but he merely stood back holding his board. "Maybe you better get behind him," he mentioned. (The art of laconic communication is an inbred country characteristic. It's in the genes.)

"Who me?"

Up ahead, Frances, legs straddling the top of the chute, commanded, "Tail him up!" I cast around in my mind. Nail him up? What did she mean?

"Grab his tail and push!"

"Oh," I murmured. Sure, why not. What was a little tail after all that mud. I grabbed a handful of curliqued rear-end appendage and shoved. Piggie advanced up the slanting chute for approximately five and a half steps. Then he retreated seven. I hung on. The hog didn't mind. He simply sat on my lap. Behind me, the farmer threw down his board and galloped to my aid. About time, I thought as I cuddled 250 pounds of lard. Squeezing in alongside me, the farmer whammed a hard fist on hoggy's backbone and shouted something outstandingly rude. Porky humphed and skedaddled up the chute with me still hanging onto his tail. Both of us fell into the strawed-down truck bed. Frances instantly dropped the stockrack gate, and the pig and I were cozily caged.

Porky immediately began chomping on some straw, and when I scratched his back again, he grunted happily.

"Gosh," I said, "this is sure a nice pig. A shame he's gotta be butchered."

"True," said Frances, "but Out West, if you want to eat it, you got to kill it first."

EDIFYING WOOLLY WEST EDICTS

Is there a correct procedure for purchasing live food from a farmer or rancher?

Answer: Sort of. It's best to bring your own truck to tote the animal away in, unless you think it will take itself to the packing plant.

Always select your own walking beef, pork or lamb. That way you've only yourself to blame for the meat you get.

Pay the livestock grower with money. He doesn't offer credit-card benefits.

Pay the livestock grower at the time of purchase. His is not a charge-account operation.

CHAPTER 13

AUCTION FEVER
(How to auct in the country)

Out West, country folks, stove up with age, illness, injury or burnout, sell their holdings to younger, stronger or richer buyers and move to town. Other oldsters, too poor to quit and too stubborn to move, keep right on keeping on until someone finds them keeled over in the barnyard, toes curled, stiff fingers clutching a pitchfork. Whatever precipitates the change in ownership, a lifetime of accumulations go on the auction block.

Newcomers are advised to work up to attending a country auction. Sashay around to a yard sale or two. Experience a church rummage before exposing yourself to a hard-core country auction. Even seasoned auction goers have been known to overdose when they see the mountains of accumulated tools, equipment, machinery, antiques, furniture, numerous mystery objects and, sometimes, puppies and kittens. Like gambling fever, auction buying inflames the brain, mesmerizing you into paying twice the price for something charmingly rusted and broken.

Mother Earthers and retired corporate magnates are especially susceptible to auction fever. One young, headbanded couple, keen on going back to the land, where they planned to can everything in sight, were seen paying $25 for ten boxes of old mayonnaise jars.

Three rich magnates competed till the highest bidder acquired a broken-down, ancient, wooden-spoked wagon that had once hauled Mother Nature's basic condiments. The rich magnate wanted to make it into a yard ornament, he said. The thing had already been a pasture ornament for 50 years. In another 50, no doubt some future nostalgia hobbyist will hang the weathered remnant above a mantelpiece.

Bidding at most country auctions begins at nine or ten a.m., so arrive early enough to look over the offerings. Dress warmly and always take along overshoes, a blanket, extra lunch and possibly a beverage for celebrating a priceless acquisition.

As you bounce over graveled country roads, be on the alert for a sawhorse that eventually appears in the middle of the driving lane. A piece of cardboard ripped from a grocery box will be nailed to the sawhorse. Handlettered in

barely visible pencil is the word ''auction.'' An equally dim
arrow points to a ranch turnoff.

Ignore designated pasture parking and ease on down
the lane until you come to a side avenue that meanders
behind the ranch house. Rein up near a small structure that
has a half moon cut in its East wall. Planning ahead is
always a good idea as comfort facilities at auctions are
likely to be tissueless. Women, especially, need to plan
ahead. Men merely stroll way out to the North 40 to inspect the big machinery. Never startle a lonesome fellow
standing on the offside of a John Deere tractor.

Once parked and conveniences scouted, find the card-
table set up either in the garage, an old sheepwagon or in
an empty granary. The auctioneer's clerk will issue you a
bidding number, a square of pasteboard marked with a
black numeral. For the rest of the day, you're not just a
name, you're a number. Wear the numeral in the crown of
your hat or protruding from breast pocket of shirt or
jacket.

Auction items are displayed in a glorious hodge-
podge, loosely categorized according to size, on three
flatbed haywagons. The variety of treasure looks like a flea
market in Zanzibar. Wagon one holds smaller items like
boxes of nails, nuts, handtools, half-used cans of paint and
antique doorknobs. Wagon two holds bigger objects such

as bundles of shingles, stacks of horsecollars, camp cots from WWI, gardening tools, wire stretchers, and 18 small motors built before the invention of electricity.

Wagon three holds cream cans, bigger motors, log chains and two-dozen ten-gallon, metal lard buckets with lids and handles. The lard buckets sell for $11 each. Nine go to the Mother Earth couple.

Piled in rows on the ground are stacks of windows and doors, spools of barbed wire, wooden panels, corral poles. . . . In the open field beyond the corrals, sickly trucks, mystery machinery and dead tractors lurk in the grass like grazing dinosaurs. Excitement increases your heart rate as you scavenge through the piles. It's a motherlode.

Besides the wares in the barnyard, there's a smorgasbord of household goods spread on trestle tables in the ranch-house yard. Sort through everything. Don't miss seeing a single old picture frame or box of dishes, stack of hand-crocheted doilies or plastic gew gaw.

Beyond the loaded tables marches an arsenal of furniture wearing the ashamed look of castoffs. Some appear to be awaiting burial. At the end of a line of mismatched, wooden kitchen chairs, two commodes and a child's desk, your heart's desire manifests itself. It is the one item you've been yearning for all your life long . . . **a treadle sewing machine in mint condition!** Be cool when you spot this incredible find. Practice nonchalance. Draw your hat down over your eyes and casually inspect the machine once, maybe twice. Try not to drool on the oak finish. Open the cute little drawers with the incised curlique decorations. Notice the elaborate scroll work on the darling foot pedal. Complete the inspection while maintaining an attitude of total nonchalance which you hope discourages competitive greed in another's heart. Shrug, then murmur in a carrying tone that no one with any intelligence would want that old thing!

When the sale begins, the raspy voiced auctioneer, who wears a cowboy hat and pointy-toed boots, gazelles onto the first wagon or stands on a chair that he then totes from place to place as he sells. From his perch, he tells bad jokes and claps his hands to josh buyers and berate slow bidders. A good auctioneer knows everybody's first name except yours.

Bidding styles vary. Some people wave their numbers and shout, "YO!" Others fix a beady eye on the auctioneer and nod slightly. Still others signal with a lifted forefinger to the cap or hat brim. Auction bidding in the Woolly West requires no previous experience, but being tall helps. Crowds of big-hatted men gather like a dense forrest close around the goodies. Women are forced to stand back peering between the few gaps in the wall of denim jackets and down vests. Shortness, an unfortunate congenital deficiency among women, causes frustration and stress. This condition can be equalized through certain techniques developed by generations of clever-thinking, auction-attending women. There is the classic, oh-I've-lost-my-contacts ploy where you fall to hands and knees and pretend to search for lost lenses, a diamond ring or car keys. Like a rabbit in the brush, hippity hop among the legs until the front-line goal is reached. This method works well on firm, dry ground, but is subject to the hazard of painfully mashed fingers.

For inclement mucky conditions, there is the tested, sidle-apology, sidle-apology, forward-edging movement, the acronym for which is "sasafe." To sasafe is to turn sideways, gently nudge the narrow touch-point between two men standing elbow to elbow, and when they glance around, sidle quickly between them, edge forward, sidle again, apologize and smile innocently. With practice you can move at the speed of an upstream-swimming salmon.

By noontime, through determined bidding, you are

the proud possessor of an antique milk can, three shovels, a log chain, 14 glass insulators, a crusty pair of leather rodent-chewed chaps you plan to hang over the fireplace alongside the rusty branding irons mounted like crossed swords over your prized acquisition, a leather framed Eddie Arnold picture.

At noon, country auctions break for lunch, a repast served from long trestle tables set up in the garage or shop building and served by the ranch wife and helpful women neighbors. Usually the food is free, a standard menu of beans, sloppy joes, potato salad and a homemade cookie. Free coffee is available all day. Sometimes lunch is served in a paper sack and consists of a rubbery slice of baloney between butterless bread and an apple. The closer to town, the stingier the lunches. Sometimes you even have to **pay**. Whether the meal is skimpy or scrumptious, unbearable hunger always strikes at three o'clock, hence the need to pack your own extra sustenance.

Move through the lunch line, collect a wobbly paper plate of sloppy joe and saunter back to the general vicinity of the soon-to-be-yours sewing machine. Country traditions says that the household goods sell immediately after lunch. This allows the women a chance to purchase items and then scurry home in time to meet the school bus, milk the cow, wash the separator and fix supper while the men continue decision-making at the sale.

Seat yourself on one of the ratty, distressed, for-sale kitchen chairs that affords a direct view of your treasure. A shiver of horror chokes the sloppy joe in your throat when you spot a purple-haired woman lurking near **your sewing machine!** Patting it. Running a greedy hand acquistively along its oak surface. The woman is an antique dealer. Anyone with purple hair, bangly bracelets, dark glasses, cigarette in a holder and wearing a stylish, beige, belted trench coat is a dead cinch to be a professional antiquer. Gloom drops over your soul like the rain that has begun to fall. Gloat that the trench-coated woman has no overshoes, and her sandaled feet are deep in cold, squishy mud. Glare at her. Maybe you can give her hives.

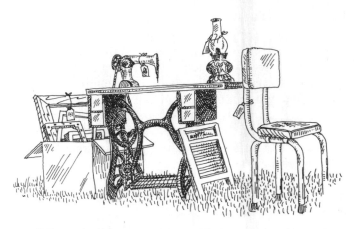

When the auction recommences, Purple Hair continues hovering. Breathe deeply to control your anxiety. Pretend to be an interested bidder and purchase a typing table that has scarcely a dent and three of its rollers are okay.

Out of an eyecorner, keep track of P.H. She is jigging and jouncing like a vulture shifting its feet. Suddenly you realize that the woman's contortions are indicative of a problem more complex than simple nervous twitch. Hope illumines your gloom.

As she nervously lights yet another cigarette, adjusts her dark glasses and crosses her legs, stroll near and join in the jiggling. Smile companionably. Then, with utmost discretion, indicate the outdoor privy a quarter mile away. Though distant, it is visible relief to anyone not willing to crouch behind a hedge.

Purple Hair, judging the distance of the auctioneer from the grail of the sewing machine, decides she can chance a trip. Be kind. Escort her around the corner and point her along the path. Then dash back to the bidding. Hope the auctioneer will get to the machine before Purple Hair and her probably limitless money returns.

Destiny is with you. All the kitchen chairs are disposed of in one bid, and the sewing machine is next. A couple of other women half heartedly bid against you, but drop out as the price goes up. When the auctioneer finally declares, "SOLD to number 71" your eyes blur. You stifle sobs as you fall across your treasure. Through the triumphal mists, you can see Purple Hair galloping back to the scene. She's too late. Too bad.

A short time later, with treasures loaded and a priceless treadle sewing machine swaddled securely under a blanket in the backend of your pickup, wave as you pass Purple Hair. Be gracious. Afford her a nice smile.

EDIFYING WOOLLY WEST EDICTS

How does a person know precisely what to bid on at a country auction?

Answer: An inner voice will guide you. When your eye falls on an object you can't live without, you will experience a gut-wrenching twinge of acquisitiveness, similar to the feeling you get an hour after eating fried zucchini. The auctioneer, who has a laser-beam sensitivity to persons suffering with Buying Fever, will exhort you to heights of bidding you'll be amazed you possess.

• • •

How many times can old tire tractors, beat up trucks or battle-scarred balers, swathers and combines be recycled through successive auctions?

Answer: No one knows. Since the invention of gasoline-fueled machinery, not one has ever been abandoned or discarded for long. Those temporarily out of operation can be found parked out back somewhere "waiting for a part" before being pressed back into service.

PART IV

WOOLLY WEST RECREATION AND SOCIAL PURSUITS

WHOOPING IT UP AT THE GIDDY-YUP CORRALS

CHAPTER 14

HORSES, HORSES, HORSES
(Advice on saddles, liniment and hay burners)

A Greenhorn's first experience on a horse Out West can be a character-building test of fortitude. Even though in your childhood back East, you've ridden many a mile atop a flat English saddle, may even have won ribbons in horse shows, you'll discover that Western horsemanship differs.

For one thing, saddles are not graceful postage-stamp bits of upholstered leather upon which the posterior reposes gracefully. No, the soft-as-a-rock Western saddle, is a deep, leather, chairlike contraption upon which the posterior bounces like a disorganized jumping bean. Stirrups the size of shoe boxes dangle from each side of the saddle. Without previous weight-lifting experience, the average Greenhorn finds it impossible to pick up the average Western saddle, whereas the true Westerner, no matter how scrawny, can one-handedly sling a saddle aboard any horse. Such expertise accounts for the prevalence of shoulder socket bursitis and slipped discs in the Woolly West.

As a newcomer eager to adapt to Woolly West ways, the opportunity to help bring in a "string of horses" thrills you to the marrow. A real cowboy adventure is at hand.

Bringing in a string of horses means starting the day before sunup. Westerners begin any outdoor venture in the pre-dawn, claiming they want to be ready when the sun rises so they can get a head start on the day. While this reasoning may not stand close logical scrutiny, it is backed by fierce Western tradition. As you lean over the corral's top rail in the gray morning light, a Western friend will bring you a horse reputed to be "gentle as a lamb", "absolutely reliable" and with a gait that's "maybe a little rough." You will be assured the four-footed hay burner has never bucked yet, giving you a slightly uneasy feeling that he is waiting till the time is right.

In the Woolly West, practically all gentle-as-a-lamb horses are a dingy, tattle-tale gray with manes and tails hanging in burr-choked clumps. While these vintage, off-white cayuses have reached an age qualifying them to be in the book of records, they are not Lone Ranger rejects. They are merely horses, that, like people, advancing years have turned their hair to silver. Your own vintage mount is called Bingo.

Before the adventure can begin, however, you must saddle up old Bingo. Pick up the ton of leather at your feet, flip the near stirrup over the saddle horn, grasp the pommel and, like a person about to put a shot, spring from bended knees, lifting at the same time and toss the saddle onto the middle of Bingo's spine. Watch out for over enthusiasm on that first toss because saddles have been known to arc high and crash to the ground on the other side of old Bingo. Seeking to adjust your throw, you may, on the next attempt, fail to heave high enough and slam the saddle into the poor horse's barrel sides. Old Bingo, having achieved his ripe age by not worrying, spraddles his feet to gain a firmer stance and hunches up for the next assault. Finally, having established the saddle in the approximate center of the patient creature's broad back, you feel proud until you realize you've forgotten to put the saddle-blanket on first. (Rumor has it there's a new strain of horses being bred, born already saddled.) There's nothing to do but start over.

At long last, blanket, saddle and cinching up accomplished in proper sequence, you are ready to commence to get on. Your heart, already strained from being forced to work at such an early hour, lurches as you gaze in dismay at the gargantuan steed looming above your head. Do not falter. Square your shoulders, beetle your brow, (a beetled brow helps hide the fright tears in your eyes), draw a deep breath. Adjust the ten gallon you're wearing to a jaunty angle, pick up Bingo's reins, lift your left foot and step into the near stirrup (the left side of the horse) and swing lightly aboard in one smooth, flowing motion. If you're a short person and the horse is tall, you may have to lift your foot higher than your head just to touch the stirrup, which makes flowing smoothly a challenge. As you claw upward you resemble a crab climbing a cliffside.

Mounting is a heap easier if you lead the horse alongside a rail fence, a car bumper, a large boulder or into a deep ditch. This method allows the rider to retain dignity.

Once in the saddle, assume immediate control to keep

Bingo's head up. His main passion is gluttony, and he is far more interested in grabbing snacks of grass, weeds and thistle tops, than in responding to your amateur commands. Each time he lunges for another horsey hors d'oeuvre, the pull on the reins wrenches your joints painfully. Keeping a short hold will help prevent Bingo's bad habit, but he never quits trying. It's easier to ride with a loose rein and let the old horse lunge at will.

As a tenderfoot, you are required to lead only one other horse, a riderless animal connected to you by a rope leading from its halter. Perhaps you've wondered why cowpunchers are often pictured wearing gloves. One experience with a rough, inch-thick hemp rope sizzling across your palms when the critter jerks back will teach you to wear sturdy leather gloves or bring an extra pair of hands.

Your fellow trail riders, each leading three or four saddleless horses, move out. As you yank up Bingo's head and move out too, it becomes obvious why old Bingo is not on the racing circuit.

For the entire journey, you will ride drag, which means the last in line and has nothing to do with kinky dress behavior. During a cattle drive, smaller calves and slow cows that can't keep up drag along behind the main bunch. Therefore the last rider "brings up the drag" or "rides drag." This position is mostly assigned to the very young, the crippled, the decrepit—or the Greenhorn.

However, drag is the perfect location from which to contemplate the fairy-tale blue of the limitless Western sky as your trusty mustang forges across brush covered rangeland. It's a pleasure to watch sagehens, spooked by the horses, take flight and skitter like water-skipping pebbles from bush to bush. Enjoy the feel of the sun warm on your back as Bingo's head bobs before you, his tacky gray mane flopping rhythmically. Keep your eyes gimleted so you can search the horizons for the occasional outlaw or maybe a roving band of hostiles or possibly a Handsome Stranger on another old white horse. Enjoy the way your lithe body balances lightly, at one with your steed's strides while the breeze slips caressing fingers through your tawny hair. Never mind whether or not your have tawny-type hair. Out West, every woman's crowning glory automatically turns tawny once she climbs on a horse. Absorb the champagne air of the real Woolly West and perhaps break into a joyful Western chorus of, "I've got spurs, that jingle, jangle, jingle. . ."

This rich fantasy-life will carry you buoyantly along for perhaps 40 minutes. Then you begin experiencing painful twinges and discover your body has stopped being lithe. It becomes evident that the earlier description of Bingo's gait as "a little rough" fell short of total accuracy, as your bones develop more jangles than the song. Besides that, the horse you are leading has decided not to wait for you. He gallops ahead, hits the end of the halter rope you're holding, and the jolt nearly flips you out of the saddle. Then the critter decides to change tactics, follows docilely for five steps, then stops dead in his tracks, nearly yanking you backwards off your precarious perch. To prevent being drawn and quartered, it's a good idea to wrap the lead rope around the saddlehorn. This may help some if you're careful not to let the rope saw a gash in your leg the next time the horse jerks back.

Try reducing the pain through meditation, all the way to unconsciousness if possible. Forget that your shoulders hurt, your knees throb, rope-burns sting your palms, and you have blistered your posterior. With your body ping-ponging on the basin of a saddle big enough to accommodate Orson Welles, trying to maintain a grip on Bingo's fat sides is about as successful as trying to clasp a wine barrel with chopsticks. With pain knifing through your knee joints, and your flopping form completely unstablized, you may be tempted to clutch the saddle horn. Shame on you. A true Westerner would fall to her death before clutching.

As the hours roll by, your stomach begins to shout that breakfast was sometime last year. Greenhorns should be aware that a Westerner, once aboard a horse, gives up eating. Therefore, to avoid slow starvation, squirrel away bits of sandwich, crackers, or even a folded over breakfast pancake. None of the riders up front will notice you back there at drag, slyly munching.

About the time you have given up hope of living to see another dawn, a halt is called to rest the **horses**. A creek gurgles nearby, and you realize your thirst is nearly equal to your leg pains. Gather together the various parts of your body, and though you try to dismount with some grace, you discover you've lost all control as your form drops like a sack of gravel. Thudding to the ground, your legs fail entirely, telescoping your torso into your boots. Save face by pretending you're merely joking. Crawl to the creek's edge, slake your thirst and then locomote to the shade of the nearest tree. Inspect the insides of your knees. Ground hamburger, surrounded by fat watery blisters, has replaced skin. Close your eyes and distract yourself by wondering if spikes have been driven between each of your spinal vertebrae. It is then you'll know why those Pioneer women **walked** alongside those wagons.

The moments of rest pass swiftly and once again it is time to mount up—a grisly prospect. But even though you know you cannot expect to survive, do not admit defeat. Stifle the moans of terminal pain and haul your tortured torso onto the saddle.

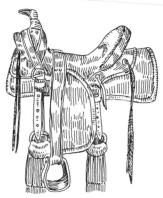

As the ordeal recommences, ease the pressure on throbbing joints and blistered knees by dangling your feet out of the stirrups. Vary that maneuver by sitting sideways, both feet flopping on one side of good old Bingo. Accept shame and cling to the saddlehorn while your abused body bops around like a rubber ball tied to a paddle. Bingo, plodding along on four flat tires and a broken axle will pay no mind to your unprofessional riding technique. He'll simply keep on clippity-clopping, clumpity-jerking along. As you try to blot out the piercing agony of each clippity, hallucinations come and go. Time warps.

It will be many days after healing up before you fully realize that you've actually helped "bring in a string of horses." By then you will also have learned that Bingo enjoys a reputation as the roughest-gaited horse in the county. For awhile you may be piqued. But all the pain will be worth it the day a visitor from Connecticut pleads to go riding. With true Western friendliness, offer to scare up a horse, gentle as a lamb, and with a gait that's maybe a little rough, by the name of Bingo. Solemnly you can assure the Greenhorn that you yourself once rode old Bingo 20 miles and he never bucked once.

EDIFYING WOOLLY WEST EDICTS

What kind of horse should a greenhorn choose to ride?
Answer: A short one unless you enjoy lifting your foot higher than your head to get on.

CHAPTER 15

HOWDY MA'AM
*(Going to a dance requires stamina,
sturdy shoes and a hollow leg)*

Socially comfortable only in the company of livestock, other men or pickups, the cowpoke, faced with a human female, behaves like a lassoed unbroken colt. He chokes, jerks back and stalks off as stiff legged as Gary Cooper at high noon.

As a Greenhorn, I yearned to become acquainted with

an honest to gosh, spur-jingling cowpoke. Frances, an experienced hand at setting bait for cowboys said the pickin's were best at a country-schoolhouse dance.

Out West, country dances remain a live whoop-it-up tradition where whole families attend, and many a single, shy Tall-in-the-Saddle has been roped in by his future mate.

On a starlit Saturday night in midsummer, Frances and I journeyed to Horse Creek School House some 35 miles up country over washboardy roads. To guarantee cowboy attention, we wore swirly-skirted dresses, high heels and clouds of perfume. It is best to avoid excessive finery, frippery, cleavage, tightage or bunnage. Shyer cowpokes, frightened by such pulchritude, may spend the evening outside peering through windows steamy from lusting hot breaths.

At Horse Creek School, we parked among randomly tethered pickups in the grassy schoolyard. My heart pitty-patted as we stepped across the threshold. Schoolhouse ambience, I discovered, was not exactly nightclubby. There were no tete-a-tete tables in darkened corners. Glaring overhead lights, bright enough for surgery, chased away every shadow. Moths threw themselves on naked lightbulbs. Rows of curtainless windows, separated by strips of white wall, grinned like sharps and flats on a keyboard. Seated on skinny benches shoved against the wall, wives, mothers, grandmothers and a few old men happily exchanged news and kept tabs on toddlers and babies. Flocks of little kids clung to their mothers until they spotted other little kids. Then, like gamboling lambs, they bunched up and started leaping and tearing around. Clumps of self-conscious giggling adolescents sashayed here and there.

Trailing after Frances, I merged with a group of bright-eyed young women clustered near a tiny, wall-mounted mirror in a far corner. All of us giggled, patted hair and darted swift glances at the herd of eligible males pawing the floor near the exit. Genuine cowboys there, I thought. Strong jawed mavericks, each one wore a pair of straight-legged, low-slung, brand new denims (that, by the end of the evening, would acquire a range-ridden look), a long sleeved snap-button western shirt, cowboy boots and a wide-brimmed western hat pulled so low on the brow the wearer had to tilt rearward to see.

Aimless, ritualistic time ticked by as the Matt Dillons and Miss Kittys fiddled, shuffled and dawdled, pretending disinterest in each other. At a beat-up piano, minus five ivories and its foot pedals, a woman piano-player tuned up with two guitars and an accordion.

Striking a chord, the band launched into "Pearly Shells." When the song ended, they played it again. And then again. At rural dances, musicians may play each tune three times in a row. No one knows why, but some speculate that repetition allows shy dancers time to make up their minds. Meanwhile, we women, bright as new crayolas, received a blizzard of sidewise looks from cowboys standing slaunch-hipped, hands in pockets, arms folded across muscular chests (all cowboys have muscular chests), staring into the atmosphere. They appeared to be tracking the flights of assorted bugs zooming around light bulbs. I watched closely, hoping to intercept one of the looks, but the bugs always won. From time to time, one cowpoke muttered to another without diverting his gaze from space. Switching hip slouches, his buddy nodded, thoughtfully extracted some snoose and took a chew. Shivers coursed down my spine. This was the real thing. Cowboys speaking cowboy.

As time passed, I became increasingly bored with hair patting and giggling. Every so often a wad of men broke off from the main bunch and went outside returning after awhile, noticeably livlier. Frances explained the mystery departures were mercy trips to pickups where the intrepid range riders heightened their social competence with a short snort. Liquor is never brought into a schoolhouse or community hall until after it's consumed. Drinking takes place outside in the fresh air as the Almighty intended. Beer and mix are kept in coolers in pickup beds or car trunks. Hard liquor is kept handy in glove compartments in case of snake bites. Out West, the medicine of choice for snakebite is whiskey. Pour three drops on anything you believe has been bitten and drink the remainder. Should the bite prove fatal, you won't care.

As the frequency of trips outside increased, the young stallions began yelling and pummeling each other. Occasionally, they would holler across at us women, who by now, were as edgy as a corral full of high-strung fillies.

Frances explained the hollering was a form of communication. "When they stop yelling," she said, "they are getting ready for an emotional commitment."

My interest quickened as I spotted a tall cowboy sporting a new straw hat so large he resembled the Flying Nun. Under the hat, his sunburned face matched his shirt.

"It's Harley, the shyest man in the country," said Frances. "He likes you, I can tell." She conferred with a paunchy individual who turned out to be one of her uncles. (In a small town every third person is kinfolk.) Uncle Paunchy listened to Frances, nodded and strolled back to the herd. Skillfully, he cut Harley away from the bunch and began easing him backwards. Meanwhile Frances jostled me forward. Eventually, our two bodies collided. Harley spun around, mashing my toe.

Through the pain I heard Uncle Paunchy perform the introductions without once mentioning my name. "Little gal visiting," was about as close as he ever got. Note to

Greenhorns: Out West, women are referred to as "she," "the girlfriend," "little gal," "her," "the wife," "the old lady," or not at all. Rural men, especially the group known as cowboys, rarely use a female's given name.

Now that Harley had come within range, he studied the floor, the ceiling, the wall behind me, anything to avoid looking at me. To help him, I became assertive, grabbed his hand (though I had to snatch it out of his pocket), and shook it vigorously.

"Howdy, Harley," I said, and mentioned my name, ennuciating slowly and clearly. Harley immediately turned the color of ketchup and retrieved his calloused, ham-sized paw.

"Er, Howdy, Ma'am." The words were muttered low at the back of his throat.

Chattily I inquired, "What's your last name, Harley?"

"Uh," said Harley.

"Your last name?" I repeated.

"Uh, Davidson," he muttered.

"Your name is Harley Davidson? Really?" I chortled, and Harley's tomatoey color deepened. He grinned sheepishly.

"Yup, uh, pleased to meet cha," he muttered, turned tail and skedaddled out the door, leaving me wondering if I had damaged his feelings.

I had no time to ponder the question. As if at a signal, suddenly everybody was dancing. Little kids, teenagers, oldsters, and all ages in-between. The floor pulsated as boot heels made punctuation marks in time to the music. The evening blossomed into a good time as several men invited me to dance. Not one removed his hat. I thought the lights had gone out before I realized a tall cowpoke-partner's exceptionally wide-brimmed hat was casting a thick shadow. Dancing with a short fellow meant cricking my neck to avoid eye-gouge.

Possible facial disfigurement wasn't the only problem. Enthusiasm often substituted for dancing ability. Sometimes I circled the room with my hand clasped by a man whose arm motion could have flagged a train. Another partner held me rigidly, stretching out my arm farther than it was meant to go while breaking trail at a gallop through the crowd.

A chunky cowboy, built like a Hereford bull, wrestled me through a specialty number called "The Shottische," which meant that every third measure, we two hopped in a circle while Chunky kicked my shins.

When the music quit, I was limping toward a bench when a Commanche yell split the air and two tall-hatted men swooped upon me. Each linked an arm through one of mine with such force, my shoulder bones threatened to separate from the sockets. Entwined, the three of us stood in a row, side by side, and began a measured heel, toe, step.

I concentrated as I copied my partners' steps. Other dancers in triad formations, also heel, toe, stepped in slow stately rthythm. What fun, I thought. This must be an old time Western folk dance. Probably handed down from early Frontier times. Abruptly the music blasted my muse as it changed tempo. The cowboy on my left, his arm hooked through mine like a chain around a log, threw his head back and ripped out a yowl that could have alerted the fort. Suddenly my feet left the floor, my body flapping like wet wash on a windy day. Marlboro Man on my left stomped in a circle, halted and dropped me. Whereupon, Hopalong Cassidy on my right, fishhooked his arm through my free elbow and stomped in a reverse circle causing my torso to whip like a rooftop weathervane. Then Hoppy quit me. Immediately Marlboro Man hooked on, and once more my feet paddled air. The frantic music slowed and again the three of us heel, toe, stepped—like finding calm water after riding the rapids. The calm was shortlived. The music burst into flame again, and my two cowpoke partners, squalling coyote yells, took turns flapping my frame in the breeze. Each time the music changed to the fast beat, it increased in speed so that by the time the dance ended on a note of yipping, yowling, laughing frenzy, the music was going lickety-split—and I had attained orbiting velocity.

My grinning partners, having worked up a terrible thirst and pleased with having shown me such a swell time, galloped away.

"That," said Frances, coming off orbit herself, "was the Butterfly Dance."

"I could tell," I said, "my wings were nearly pulled off."

As I dizzily aimed for a bench hoping for a few moments respite, Harley appeared. Even in my weakened condition, I noticed a definite personality change. A catfish grin pasted across his face, Harley drew closer and asked, "Ja like t'dance?"

Pleased, but slightly off balance, I fell into his arms. Harley choked and jerked back. Holding me close as a ten-foot pole, he steered me around the floor, his left hand pulverizing my right. I shouted pleasantries across to him, but conversation was difficult from half a block away. He grinned and reddened and grinned and grinned. We two-stepped around the room as the band played "Blueberry Hill." (Two-stepping is a rural dance step that grew out of the Western habit of carefully picking up and setting down feet in corrals.)

When "Blueberry Hill" ceased for the third time, Harley, deathgripping my hand in his, trotted toward the exit, pulling me along. What now? Was I being hauled off to his cave, like Tarzan with Jane? No, I was being invited on one of those mystery trips. Harley also invited Frances and a blonde cowboy named Orval who had been peering at her from behind a post. Outside, I galloped along through the tall grass. Stickery begger-lice barnacled my nyloned legs, and I discovered first hand, or first foot, that the schoolyard was also a cow pasture. Our patrol halted next to a yellow pickup. Harley opened the door, flipped open the jockey box and pulled out a bottle of spirits as big as a fire hydrant.

Removing the cap, he handed the jug first to Orval who tipped it up and swallowed and swallowed. A sigh of deepest pleasure escaped his lips. Orval then offered the beverage to Frances, who did not hesitate. She winked at me, slanted the jug and appeared to swig down the liquid. Must be tasty, I thought. Then it was my turn and Harley spoke his second sentence of the evening. "Have some," he said, wiping the bottle on his sleeve and handing it to me.

Frances, whom I considered my good friend, smiled, wide eyed, winked again and instructed me to take a big-g-g swallow. Reminding myself that alcohol kills germs, I lapped my lip around the bottle top. My throat opened and a blend of acid, vinegar and swamp water cauterized my gullet. Tears streamed from my eyes. The insides of my cheeks burned, and the need to spit puckered me unattractively. Gasping, I poked the jug blindly at Harley, catching him in the mid-section. Harley never noticed. He accepted the jug and guzzled as though he'd just come in off the desert.

Another round started. Orval took a slug and handed the bottle to Frances who flashed me another exaggerated wink, tipped 'er up and gulped. I figured her amazing capacity must have something to do with being reared in the Woolly West.

The community jug came to me again.

"Finish her off," drawled Harley, again sanitizing the top with his sleeve. Gazing hard at my friend, I silently begged her help, but she only winked once more. Resigned to death by alcohol poisoning, I swallowed more raw booze, wondering if Frances knew she had a tic in her left eye.

As we returned through the weeds and cowpies to the school room, the music ceased, and a few beats later, people stopped dancing. Outside folks came in, and inside folks stayed in. At the far end of the room, a panel had been opened, revealing a kitchen. Spread out on the pass through counter were boxes and plates of sandwiches, cakes, cookies and a giant urn of coffee. The crowd formed a line, and Frances guided me in behind Harley and Orval. I was grateful for the help because my arms and legs were missing.

"Frances," I whispered, "I don't feel so well."

"You should have done what I did," said Frances. "I just pretended to drink. You're supposed to sort of blow bubbles back into the bottle which makes everybody **think** you're drinking. I tried to clue you. That's why I kept winking."

"Oh," I said. "I thought you'd hurt your eye."

"You'll be fine as soon as you get something to eat," said my practical friend, shoving me along in line.

At the sandwich counter, a cowboy was holding his hat upside down before him. It was the first time that evening I'd seen a bareheaded man, and I ducked my head, embarrassed. Both Harley and Orval tossed money into the fellow's hat. "Frances," I whispered, "is he needy?"

Frances explained that the hatholder was collecting

donations to pay the musicians. Women didn't contribute because they brought the food.

Frances helped me pile sandwiches and cake on a paper plate. She filled cups with strong black coffee, and we staked a claim on a bench. I discovered I was starving. Harley sat close to me with only Frances and Orval between us. Frances whispered such proximity indicated Harley was truly smitten. I didn't know how she could tell. There was no small talk. The two men each wolfed down 17 half-sandwiches, a gallon of coffee and a couple of pounds of cake. That took maybe ten minutes. Appetites sated, they rose, dumped their plates into trash boxes and eased toward the exit. Glassy, fervent expressions radiated across their countenances.

"Where are they going now, Frances?" I asked.

"Outside for a drink."

I shuddered. "Don't include me," I whispered. "I think that vodka was poisoned."

"That wasn't vodka," corrected Frances. "That was 100-proof grain alcohol."

Harley had trudged almost to the door when he about-faced and hollered, "C'n I call ya?"

Stupified, I nodded, and Harley's catfish grin threatened to dislocate his ears. Then he whirled and trotted after Orval.

"Congratulations," said Frances, "you've hooked a cowboy."

"I have?" I murmured, too befogged to care.

"Yep," she said, "and I'm going to show you how to reel him in."

EDIFYING WOOLLY WEST EDICTS

To which country Community Hall or Schoolhouse dances do you take sandwiches or cake?

Answer: All of them, whether they're held in your county or not.

•●•

What time does a country dance end?

Answer: Usually within a day or so after it starts.

—●—

CHAPTER 16

WOOLLY WEST COURTING PRACTICES
(Throwing a loop on that lonesome bachelor can be stressful)

Acceptable romance in the Woolly West requires two persons, one male and one female, and no approximations.

A typical first-date courting event may be a movie in a town, somewhere within a 150-mile radius. The occasion actually begins about an hour past the appointed time with the discovery that Harley has been sitting outside in his pickup staring at the house. Sometimes only the pickup is there. Harley is uptown gathering courage. Leaving behind his beloved pickup is a sure sign he'll be back.

Control impatience. Read "Gone With The Wind" or three Silhouette Romances. Sooner or later Harley will come shuffling to the door, his best going-to-town Stetson shoved to the back of his head and a wide, wall-eyed grin splitting his face. Occasionally he carries hat in hand. If so, take a good look. It's likely the last opportunity you'll get to check out his hair for color, texture and plentitude.

Dating a Western male can be hazardous, especially in high heels. Climbing unaided—and **unaided** is the way it's going to be—into a pickup truck tends to destroy that delicate superfeminine image you've spent hours acquiring. Baling strings piled like a nest of cobras on your side of the pickup floor, briar patch your nyloned legs. Debarking may become a test of savoire faire and dignity if a heel catches in the twine. Dragging a string behind you for a block and a half can be embarrassing, and Harley would never be rude enough to mention your following. He'll think it's part of your feminine mystique.

On subsequent dates, you will know to wear jeans and sturdy shoes because once Harley is used to you, he will take you along to pitch hay to the cows or take salt blocks to the North 40. You'll never again see the opening scenes of a movie, so it's best to read the book, otherwise you'll never understand why Rhett informs Scarlett, "Frankly, my dear, I don't give a damn."

ROMANCE LANGUAGE

When Wade or Clyde or Harley comes a-courtin', how will you, the Greenhorn female person recognize a compliment?

. . . He'll compare your hair to the mane on his sorrel horse.

. . . He says you make him feel as frisky as a newborn calf on spring grass.

How will he let you know he's thinking of you?

. . . He'll show up at your residence in town at 6 a.m. on a Saturday morning (the day you and the neighbors sleep in) with a cattle-truck full of bawling calves. He is surprised when the neighbors complain and even more surprised you aren't up.

. . . He drops in unannounced and eats the entire roast you've planned to last all week.

How does Tall-in-the-Saddle entertain you when out on an actual date?

. . . At a dance, he parks you in a booth, along a wall, or on a barstool and then stands in an opposite corner with a herd of other men.

. . . He is puzzled when you get huffy at being left alone.

. . . He doesn't realize you are left alone.

. . . He thinks putting you out to graze with the other fillys is company enough.

. . . He becomes angry if some other man asks you to dance.

. . . He becomes angrier if you accept.

How does a Woolly Westerner show you he values your company beyond measure?

. . . He asks you for a date and then drives over hill and bumpy dale pointing out cattle, haycrops, the old homestead, the new homestead and the place where the brockle-faced cow fell in the bog.

What happens when a cowboy (having come to town to purchase a tractor part) thinks to ask you to lunch?

. . . He escorts you to a hamburger-stand lunch counter.

. . . During the entire meal, he talks to the rancher seated on his other side.

What is the high point of a country Western courtship?

. . . As a special treat, Tall-and-Silent takes you to a bull-auction sale in February, and you're dressed in thin polyester. For hours you sit slowly congealing on slab-cold bleachers.

How do you know when Handsome Cowpoke is becoming passionate?

. . . After eight dates or three months, whichever comes first, he finally kisses you goodnight.

How do you know when he's really becoming dead serious about you?

. . . He invites you to meet his parents and they invite 85 relatives to meet you.

. . . He invites you to his ranch and shows you a basket overflowing with 300 unmated socks.

    You realize your own heart is lost when you begin pairing them.

EDIFYING WOOLLY WEST EDICTS

Is it true that Out West, there are bachelors galore in them thar hills?

Answer: Yes.

•●•

Is there a way to coax the bachelors out of the hills?

Answer: No.

•●•

Do they ever emerge at all?

Answer: Yes. To pay taxes, to ship the calves, sell the lambs, purchase a part for the swather or to attend a funeral. (Their own.)

CHAPTER 17

SATURDAY NIGHT IN A COWTOWN CAN'T BE BEAT

(An absolutely true account—only the names are changed to protect the guilty)

Scattered in the outer hinterlands of ranch country are tiny cowtowns whose cultural and business centers consist of a saloon and a general store with three gas pumps out front. Deceptively quiet all week, when Saturday rolls around, the towns roar into action. Frances said you can't beat Saturday night in a cowtown. She claimed that hordes of cowboys, starving for culture and recreation, converge on the saloon every Saturday night.

To meet some culturally inclined cowpokes, Frances and I set out one bright, sunny Saturday. We drove a hundred miles along a narrow, blacktop road. I was beginning to doubt the existence of any kind of hamlet when there, beneath the technicolor-blue sky, we came upon a flotsam scattering of buildings. Around the lonesome structures, a sea of hayfields and rangeland flowed to distant mountains.

Frances halted the car before a two-story false-front edifice of peeling, white-painted clapboard. Letters above its entry bragged "Hotel" and "Eats." Snuggled to the Hotel's side like a ragtag brother was a log building, gleaming a soft orange in the late afternoon sunlight. From the eves, a swinging signboard announced, "Saloon" and in the window, glowing neon letters spelled, "Beer."

"We're here," said Frances.

"Where?" I asked. Warm sunshine glinted off the car hood, cooking my elbow where it stuck out the window. The only signs of life were a couple of bees bobbing around a dandelion, a few flies scrambling across the saloon's screen door and a grasshopper spitting up on a weed. Grave doubts regarding the evening's entertainment quality stirred in my breast.

Inside the Saloon's dim interior, two men occupied bar stools. The taller man, who heartily bid us welcome, turned out to be the proprietor. He insisted we were in for a big time.

The second man looked like a banty rooster, roosting. His skinny legs were bent double so that scruffy boot heels could snag on the top rung of the barstool. Two barely separated beady eyes glittered in a lined, stubblebearded face, and a dirt-crusted hat swallowed his cranium. Only his outstanding, hayhook proboscis prevented his hat from slipping to his shoulders. To see, he had to tip back. I surmised that he had been culturally deprived for a long time. With a voice like steel wool scratching on a tin skillet, he introduced himself as "Shorty, the Sheepherder," and, with a wink at me, picked up a shot glass and tossed whiskey down his throat without touching glass to lips. Gloomily I wondered if Shorty represented Western macho man.

As the sun began to set, a few cowboys and hayhands, freshly scrubbed and shaved, trickled into the Saloon. They stomped, scuffed, and howdy'd the bartender, but ignored us females. Frances seemed unconcerned. She and Shorty struck up a conversation about sheep and the best way to eliminate "them blankety-blank sheep-eating coyotes." I nursed a drink and stared at a bread-board size glass box resting on a shelf next to the cashew nuts. Inside the box was a stuffed animal, an exotic creature with two horns growing from its forehead. Frances said it was a jackalope. She said winters were long in those parts and jackrabbits grew so big some years, they mated with antelopes.

A young couple entered the Saloon, slipped into a corner booth that was upholstered in plastic pinto, and melted into an endless embrace. Small bunches of gussied-up young women breezed in and took strategic command posts. Older couples, more at ease with life, relaxed at the half dozen tables scattered the length of the room.

As more cowboys entered, some distinctly Marlboro types, my spirits lightened. Sidelong glances confettied over Frances and me, but not a soul tried to introduce himself. I wondered if we would sit there all evening experiencing nothing but furtive ogling. Men lined the bar, hats shoved back, boot heels hooked on the rail. I heard "that old bronc sunfished on me " and "that blamed heifer . . ." and "you shoulda seen old Bill let loose of that haybale when that there rattler slid out . . ." Ah, I thought, the sounds of real Woolly West talk.

Drinks stockpiled in front of Frances and me as bashful cowboys, too scared to converse, kept the bartender busy bringing us refreshments. Cowboys may be shy, but they won't allow anyone to expire from thirst. Caution: Having a drink bought for you does not constitute a commitment on the cowpoke's part or yours. Western men buy drinks for women because, like mountains, they are there.

Under no circumstances should you gallop over and start a conversation or join the drinkbuyer. A gift drink requires no response other than to instruct the bartender to extend your thanks. While this may seem a slow way to initiate an acquaintance, that's the way it is Out West. Do not feel obliged to consume the extra beverages before you. Brain damage could result. At about free drink number seven, it's okay to nod and smile directly at whichever cowboy you think you prefer. If he nods and smiles back, you've got a relationship started . . . maybe.

My attention was distracted from the jackalope by the arrival of the live music, a family group. They gathered near a beat-up piano where Mom rippled some chords, Dad picked guitar, and junior, a kid about 14, blew a silver-colored tin kazoo shaped like a bugle. He played creatively, tilting the instrument up on high notes and swooping down on low. "Red River Valley" was indistinguishable from "Home on the Range," but nobody cared.

The clamor increased. Drinks flowed faster. Cowboys, having imbibed quarts of courage, began to toss questions at us and volunteer their names. They clustered around, holding drinks and grinning. Pretty soon, braver individuals separated from the herd, invited us to dance, and love began to flower in Marlboro hearts. Three different men invited me to leave the bar and go for a walk. Frances said that was a compliment as cowboys never walk. Two others coaxed me to meet their mothers. Four assorted Tall-in-the-Saddles offered to teach me how to rope a calf, and I received one and a half proposals of marriage. The half was from a man passionately proclaiming he planned to wed me as soon as his divorce became final.

A baby-faced cowpoke Frances dubbed "Durwood," wearing a blue-plaid shirt with the new creases still in it, a 60-gallon hat and a red neckerchief, fell in love with both of us. Durwood spoke little, just panted heavily and hauled us, alternately, onto the dance floor to stumble through steps invented on the spot.

During Frances' turn I watched as he pumphandled around the crowded room, taking giant knee-lifted strides that had no relation to the music's beat. Other dancers scattered as he plowed amongst them, inflicting pain. When the music quit, Durwood drew rein and returned Frances to her barstool. I thought I heard her vertebrae clicking back in place.

The next tune started and Durwood reached for me. I stalled. "You have a horse, Durwood?" I asked, desperately.

"Name's not Durwood," he stated.

"Oh, I call everybody Durwood I truly like." I prattled on. "You know, Durwood, I surely would like to see a real cowpony. I'm sorry you didn't bring yours. I've heard handsome cowboys ride their cayuses into bars. Is that true?"

Durwood looked puzzled. Then his slack mouth tightened into a wide grin. Nodding as though remembering a secret, he turned and galloped away, blue plaid elbows flapping.

Frances and I gratefully gave our feet a respite. As I turned to speak to her, I saw a camel. It was plodding through the front door.

"Frances," I asked, "on what do cowboys ride the range in these parts?"

She swung around to see what I was gaping at. "Oh," she said calmly, "that's Honey Baby. She belongs to the bartender. Some say he traded his wife for the camel on account of she disappeared right after the camel arrived."

Shouts of happy recognition emanated from the crowd, but the dromedary's owner seemed put out. As the beast moseyed further inside, a body could be seen plastered to its hump. It was Durwood. The camel, paying no attention to her passenger, plodded along snuffling at beer cans. Her angry master stomped from behind the bar. "Git off my camel," he roared. Reaching up, he peeled Durwood off. Honey Baby continued her stroll, salivating on glasses and scarfing potato chips and peanuts. Frances and I retreated as the advancing beast began slurping our back-logged drinks.

Grabbing the camel's lead rope, the saloon owner moaned, "Honey Baby, come with Papa." Honey Baby snorted nastily and spat on Shorty's hat. I realized that Shorty, a reliably steady drinker, had never moved from his perch. I whispered to Frances, "How come he never has to go?"

"Some say," she answered, "sheepherders don't."

We dodged away from Honey Baby as she nuzzled Shorty's crusty headgear again. Shorty, angered, swept it off, revealing a shiny pate, spider tracked with half a dozen hairs. Whopping the camel, he croaked, "Git outta here, you miserable varmint!"

The camel kissed Shorty's bald pate and belched. Her master, hanging on to the halter rope, dug in his heels. Ponderously, the sway-necked beast reversed direction, allowing her owner to lead her back through the cheering crowd, who patted her barrel sides and offered her more beer. Durwood, pleased with himself, swept me onto the dance floor.

A number of drinks and a lot of dancing later, the crowd thinned. The kazoo, guitar and piano player left. Only the couple in the corner booth remained locked in the same embrace. Frances and I agreed we were in no shape to drive home safely. We decided to book a room at the inn.

The bartender, who was also the innkeeper, assured us there was a vacancy. He led us through a connecting door into the hotel building, up some creaky, wooden stairs and along a dark hallway. A door opened, a light switch clicked. Weak illumination from a single ceiling bulb showed a small square, room with two tall windows, the uncurtained panes ink-dark and staring. The room was functionally furnished with a double bed, a dresser and one straight-backed chair. A row of hooks on a board served as a closet. On the high, old-fashioned, curliqued bedstead, a homemade, rainbow-quilted counterpane glowed.

"Bathroom's at the end of the hall," said the innkeeper. "Ain't no locks on these here doors, girls, but you'll be fine. Ain't nobody else around."

Frances and I were too tired to be concerned. We shut the door and stuck the straight backed chair under the knob. I yanked off my boots, peeled down to basic underwear, and spread shirt and jeans on the dresser. Frances slipped out of her shirt and smoothed it across the chair seat, figuring it would stay fairly wrinkle free. Then she placed her jeans neatly across the foot of the bed where they'd be handy come morning. As I crawled in on the far side of the bed, I noticed the blackness outside had turned murky gray. Frances snapped off the light at the wall switch and scooted under the covers. Both of us sighed gratefully as the fluffy mattress cradled our fatigued bodies, and the thick quilted comforter cocooned around us.

I prepared to welcome blissful unconsciousness. "'Night, Frances," I murmured. Suddenly I felt something crawling on my arm. Something slimey. I flung back the covers, searching for a loathesome interloper. In the dimness, I could see nothing, so I reached over and swatted Frances. "There was a snake in this bed!" I babbled hysterically. "It crawled over my arm!"

Frances, knowing I was an uneducated ignorant Greenhorn, was patient and understanding. "Don't be a noodlehead," she said, "there are no snakes here. You're hallucinating. Go to sleep!"

In the face of such firmness, I thought she must be right. The tickling was probably just a loose piece of yarn from the quilt ties. Maybe I was developing D.T.'s from too much camel-tainted whiskey. I sank back under the covers. All was silent. Mists of unconsciousness floated across my brain. Then, once more, something wriggled along my forearm. I shot to a sitting position and socked Frances again. Her eyes flew open, and I saw murder lurking there. But I was not to be deterred. Unreasoning terror gripped me. I shook her with both hands. "Snake, snake!" I babbled.

Frances' patience came to an end. "We," she said, her voice guillotine sharp, "are on the second floor of an hotel. A snake would have to be damned enterprising to make the journey all the way up here." Gently she added, "NOW SHUT UP AND GO TO SLEEP!"

With that she clutched her half of the covers around her ears, did a big flopturn so she landed facing outward, as far away from me as she could, warning that if I struck her again, it was going to strain our friendship. Banging her head on the pillow, she dug in, grumbling like an irritated mole. Then she chanced to glance down. Protruding from beneath the bed was a blue-plaid shirtsleeve with an arm in it. Her grumbles ceased abruptly, and for 15 seconds, she did not move or breathe. I sensed something was terribly wrong.

Cautiously, she rolled onto her back muttering, sotto voice, "There's somebody's arm under the bed. Don't move." Slowly, like Dracula from his coffin, Frances rose to a sitting position and hoisted her legs from under the bedclothes. Sneaking a hand to the foot of the bed she grasped her jeans, cautiously shrugged into them and softly slid her leather belt out of the loops. Carefully, she established herself on her knees on top of the covers.

In the increasing light, I could see scratch marks on the bedstead and the way one iron spoke bent to one side. My friend gingerly kneewalked to the foot of the bed. Taking a wrap on the tongue end of her belt, she left the brass-buckle end swinging free. Like Wonder Woman tossing her lasso, Frances slammed down on the protruding arm. It spasmed and she bellowed, "Get out of there, you son of a bitch!"

"Owww," a voice whimpered.

Frances did not stop with one blow. As fast as she could swing, she whipped the arm. It disappeared under the bed. Leaning down, she slashed sideways, and there was a satisfying thonk as the buckle connected with a hard skull.

"Yiiii!" howled the voice. We heard a frantic scrabbling and, on my side, between bed and wall, a head blooped up like toothpaste from a tube. The head still had its cowboy hat and was followed by a pair of blue-plaid shoulders. Since there was only a foot of available space, the attached body was semi-trapped. With a Tarzan yell, and whirling her belt, Frances leaped atop the bed where I sat huddled, covers modestly clutched. She bounded around me, belt sizzling. Some of the blows missed the target, but not all.

Blue-Plaid yelled and blooped out of sight again. With an acrobatic trampoline bounce, Frances spun around in midair, rebounded and caught him as he emerged from under her side of the bed.

"DON'T HIT ME LADY, PLEASE DON'T HIT ME!" Throwing a protective arm across his face, he rose as far as his knees and folded his hands in fervent plea. Frances showed no mercy.

"Get out, get out, you son of a bitch!" In her anger, she was growing repetitive.

Blue-Plaid yelped again. "OWWWW! OK, LADY, OK, OK!" Scrambling like a pup on a slick floor, he lurched to his feet, stumbled toward the door and fell on the propped chair where Frances had so tidily placed her shirt.

"GET OFF THERE!" Frances screeched, lashing him again. The fellow, using both hands to protect his face, began to sob. Tears ran down his cheeks and dripped off his chin.

Managing to turn around, shoulders hunched against pelting blows, he shoved the chair aside and clawed open the door. Trying to exit, he caught his boot toe on the door frame, crashed to his knees and Toulouse Lautreced down the corridor. Frances slammed shut the door and stood there, arm upraised, just in case. Her mouth hung open, her breath rattled in the lengthening silence.

I could see goose bumps prickling her bare arm, where it poised in the air. Her naked toes curled up from the cold splintery floor. Still clutching covers to my bosom, I began to giggle. Frances turned to find me pointing like Saca-jawea at the door. "Th . . . tha . . . that was Durwood!" I fell into a whooping hyena screech.

Frances lowered her arm. She was still angry. She looked under the bed in case Durwood had brought a friend, stuck the chair back under the knob and hopped back under the covers.

I flopped flat out, choking with laughter. "That snake!" I sputtered. "The snake was old Durwood with lust in his heart. He must have slipped his clammy hand under the covers and tickled my arm."

Frances, calm now, snuggled under the bedclothes, and broke up too. She whooped. She wheezed. She whomped her fist on her pillow. "Did you see that devil run? High-tailed it outta here like a scalded dog. Never even lost his hat."

Gasping, we reviewed the snake's discovery and expulsion once more. Tears of merriment dribbled into my ears. Between choking fits of laughter, I sputtered, "I have to admit, Frances, you're absolutely right. Saturday night in a cowtown can't be beat!"

EDIFYING WOOLLY WEST EDICTS

In a Western cowtown, what time does its only saloon lock up?

Answer: Dawn or never, whichever comes first.

CHAPTER 18

ELBOW BENDING

*(Where to find comradeship, hire a hand or
talk to a sheepherder)*

In the Woolly West, tampering with a person's right to tipple is nearly as hazardous as tampering with his or her right to bear arms. While many people abstain from alcohol consumption entirely, Out West, teetotalers and non-teetotalers respect each others preferences . . . as long as they don't drive or abuse the horses while indulging. Statistically, the number of saloons in a small town equals the number of church denominations, so that devout individuals may worship wherever they choose.

Types of establishments devoted to imbibing and relaxing fall into a particular pattern in small Western towns. There's always one drinking/eating enterprise that strives for a posh but friendly ambience. It's always called "The Wagonwheel," "The Spur," or "The Starlight Lounge." In the dining room, a stone fireplace with an ox yoke, crossed branding irons, a Moose head or all three will be mounted above the mantel. You can tell the food is gourmet because the lettuce salad has slivered carrots sprinkled over, and on Mother's Day, the napkins are cloth.

Down the block, another emporium, always called "The Oasis," "The Timber," or "The Stockman", sells three kinds of sandwiches—ham and cheese, ham and pickle or ham. Two doors farther on, Burt's Bar merchandises booze, with jerky and salted nuts the only form of solid nourishment. When hunger strikes, imbibers trot back up the street to The Timber.

Harder to find, across the tracks and tucked between the hardware store and the empty warehouse, Tiny's Tavern caters to the transient, the homeless, the habituals and the slumming. Referred to as "Sheepherder's Heaven," it's a therapeutic center where broken down herders and cowpunchers can buy liquid comfort, boiled eggs, pickled eggs, pickled turkey gizzards and occasionally sandwiches heated in a countertop oven. Comradery and all creature comforts come with the price of a drink at Tiny's, including the use of a hard bench in the back room to sleep it off.

In any of the beverage parlors, ordering a drink is simple, as Western bartenders rarely pour anything more complicated than whiskey and water. If you feel you want something fancy, you can request an olive.

Out West, there is no social pressure to choose one saloon over another. The choice is yours, and status or economic level have no bearing on the welcome you'll receive, although thirsty folks tend to fall into predictable groupings.

Burt's Bar, for instance, is headquarters for out of work cowhands, the local junk man and, after four o'clock, the men schoolteachers. At five o'clock, the businessmen, clerks and car salesmen also stop at Burt's for an emotional lift.

The Wagonwheel or Starlight Lounge entertains homemakers relaxing after a Tupperware party, a ceramics class, or a PTA meeting, and women schoolteachers (but this last group only on Friday afternoons).

While ties, dress jackets or other formal attire are not required in any establishment, proprietors do insist on shoes and shirts. These requirements have occasionally frustrated some hippies and back-to-earthers. Should you be a shirtless, shoeless person, borrow a suitable garment and strap rags to your feet. Otherwise, your thirst will remain unquenched unless you want to dip into the dogs' dish.

Greenhorns should be aware that disparaging, haughty, patronizing or snobbish manners in any beverage parlor is not a good idea. The fellow wearing the dusty hat and shredded Levis tossing back a whiskey and water may be the mayor, the county commissioner or the rancher who owns the piece of land you wish to purchase.

Bars, taverns and saloons Out West are not only social centers, they also double as employment offices. Transient and itinerant ranch hands belly up to the bar and nurse a beer as they wait to be plucked off the vine. The rancher needing temporary hired help may journey into town hoping to find a body able enough to stack hay, or possibly operate an irrigating shovel. If the twain meet, they exchange vows and drive off together in the rancher's pickup. Frequently, the newly hired hand is discharged and hauled back to town within a day or so, either because he is surprised to learn he's actually expected to work or occasionally wash, or because he's had a haybale chock full of rattlesnakes flung at him atop the stack.

Such surprises drive a man to drink.

EDIFYING WOOLLY WEST EDICTS

What is a sheepdog?

Answer: A four-footed, medium-sized friendly cannine who spends time herding sheep and waiting outside bars for his master.

• ● •

How should you behave in a Woolly West bar?

Answer: You don't have to behave in a Woolly West bar.

• ● •

What is a ditch?

Answer: a) A gully in the earth often filled with irrigating water.

b) Whiskey or bourbon and water—what you get served when you ask for a drink in a Woolly West bar.

• ● •

Besides a ditch, what other drinks are served in a bar Out West?

Answer: Vodka and orange juice, and beer. For anything else you have to bring along your own recipe and sometimes the ingredients as well.

• ● •

What happens to the Greenhorn who asks for a Manhatten, a martini or a daiquiri?

Answer: You receive a puzzled look and a ditch with a cherry in it.

CHAPTER 19

POWDER RIVER, LET 'ER BUCK!
(Spine-tingling takes on new meaning)

Spain and Mexico have bullfights. The Wild Woolly West has Rodeos; sporting entertainments wherein men and women of amazing courage compete in bull riding, bronc riding, calf roping, team roping, bull dogging—all events that require a great deal of strength, agility, and a genuine love of plowing the ground with your face.

In the animal-riding events, a contestant is required to climb aboard an untamed animal that has been tightly cinched around its rear quarters. The creature hates this indignity and therefore attempts to dislodge the rider and kill him if possible. The aim of the game is for the rider to stay in the middle of the animal's back for a count of eight seconds. After that a whistle blows and the cowboy may get off, a feat usually accomplished very quickly as the horse or bull wants to assist the dismounting by slamming the rider into the turf.

HOW TO TELL WHAT'S GOING ON AT A RODEO

GRAND ENTRY: At the start of the festivities, an announcer situated in a booth high above the arena welcomes the crowd, tells some excruciatingly bad shaggy dog stories and finally announces the Grand Entry. Instantly a tape-recorded band blares out a Sousa march, a gate swings open at the far end of the arena, and a river of riders gallop in and rein up in front of the grandstand.

Then two riders, one bearing Old Glory and one proudly carrying the State Flag, "ride the colors." The flag bearers spur their horses into a gallop and race in opposite directions around the perimeter of the arena, halting once more in front of the grandstand. The taped music changes to "The Star Spangled Banner" and the announcer declares, "Ladies and gentlemen, our national anthem!" With hands over hearts, the audience joins in singing the anthem, all but the high notes.

Next, the announcer introduces all the important riders presently in the rodeo limelight. The crowd applauds each name. Clowns are introduced. The crowd applauds. Trick riders are singled out. The crowd applauds. Local persons of note and the Rodeo Queen are announced and the crowd applauds. Finally, all introductions completed, the flag bearers once more ride the colors and finish by leading the whole troop out of the arena. It's a fine sight to see fifty or sixty horses and riders galloping gloriously through clouds of choking dust while Sousa blares through the speakers.

BRONC RIDING: In this event, the horse gets to wear a saddle and the rider gets to try to sit on it for eight seconds. For any of the riding events, the animals to be ridden must be maneuvered into the bucking chutes. Narrow, wooden enclosures, just wide enough and long enough for one horse or one bull at a time, the chutes each have a gate that will swing open to spill out the animal before the admiring audience.

A bronc rider aiming to place himself aboard a saddle-bronc straddles the chute from above, then gingerly lowers himself onto the horse's back, slips his feet into the stirrups, takes a wrap on the halter rope with one hand and shouts "Turn 'er loose!" Or, "Powder River, let 'er buck!" That's the signal for a couple of cowboys tending the gate to swing it open. Instantly, the horse lunges out, wildly intent on ridding itself of the odius creature on its back. Snorting, bucking, sunfishing, the bronc gives no quarter, but then neither does the cowboy. Between jumps he tries his best to spur the enraged cayuse to greater frenzy.

Most bronc riders wear flappy chaps, often fringed, often insigniaed with their own or their girlfriend's initials. The purpose of the flapping chaps is to increase the horse's yearning to pitch his rider into the next county. While all this pitching and bucking is going on, the cowboy is not allowed to hold onto anything but the thick halter rope clutched in one hand. His other hand must be stuck in the air as though he's trying to flag a train. The severity of the bronc's thunderous jolts causes the airborne hand and arm to flop. Mad is the cowboy whose free hand drops and touches any part of the horse. He'll be penalized points and may then be "out of the money." Rodeo events are scored according to a point system. The individual collecting the most points wins the "purse" or "top money." Sometimes the amount is considerable enough to pay for the accumulated bruises, broken bones, wrenched muscles.

During all the commotion of snorting, bucking horse, and spurring, flopping rider and cheering crowd, two men on the ground scrutinize the action. They carry clipboards and gravely mark a score on each rider's performance, the scoring based on severity of the animal's bucking, the rider's speed of spurring, and whether or not he jabbed his spurs the moment the bronc erupted from the chute. To do that, the cowboy had to have had his feet poised to bring his spurs down just ahead of the animal's shoulders. If the rider misses jabbing the horse, he "goose eggs" and therefore loses points.

If all goes well and the rider stays aboard the full eight seconds, he then has permission to stop spurring and dismount. However, since no one has informed the horse of the plan, the critter goes right on bucking wildly. At this point, a man on a broke horse rides in close alongside the pitching bronc and attempts to scoop off the rider. It's a little like a knight rescuing a maiden off a dragon . . . sort of. If the rescue man or "pickup rider" fails to snag the bronc rider, the latter individual has several options. He can wait around for another rescue attempt by the pickup man, or he can leap off and try to land on his feet like Superman. Or he can cling to the saddle horn, try to keep himself from being accidently neutered, and wait till the critter careens into a fence. At the auspicious moment he makes a leap for the top rail where he clings like a fly, allowing the horse to go its separate way. Or he can just fall off, taking his chances that nothing he is fond of will break. Everytime a pickup rider does manage to pluck a cowboy off a still bucking bronc, the crowd cheers. Everybody loves a successful rescue.

BAREBACK RIDING: This is not an event wherein the rider is unclothed, but refers to the fact that the horse wears no saddle. The cowboy, while holding onto the halter rope with one hand, must attempt to balance aboard a naked bucking horse for eight seconds. Again the rider must spur the horse in the shoulders when first emerging from the chute. He must not allow his free hand to touch horseflesh. Authorities claim that staying on a bareback bronc is more difficult than staying on a saddle bronc. The same authorities admit that the bareback rider avoids the possibility of catching a boot in a stirrup, getting hung up like a caught fish and being dragged, head down, at full gallop through the dirt while the frenzied bronc trys to kick his skull in.

BULL RIDING: This event can be the most exciting of all because unlike horses who will usually run off once they get rid of their riders, bulls will spin around and try to gore the fallen human. This makes for alert cowboys.

To distract the bulls from their prey, rodeo clowns, (men dressed in funny clothes and wearing makeup) run in front of the critter the second it dumps its rider. When the animal turns on him, the clown jumps into a barrel and cowers while the bull gores it time after time. Some say this is where the term "horning in" originated. Sometimes both the terrified cowboy and the clown are chased over the nearest fence by a snorting, raging bull. The crowd cheers enthusiastically when no one gets hurt. Should the bull catch up with one of the men, the crowd will cheer even louder when the bull-tossed man gets up and staggers off under his own power. If the ambulance takes him out the arena, he receives an ovation lasting for several minutes. Anyone who gets hurt is considered to have been terribly brave and deserving of warm applause.

BULL DOGGING OR STEER WRASSLING: In the bull - dogging event, the animals aren't really bulls anymore, so steer wrassling (a Western word akin to

"wrestling") is a more apt term. The creatures are chosen for their long, spikey horns. The dogger, a man of admirable courage and terrific tolerance for pain, plus another rider, gallop flat out alongside a steer, forming a moving alleyway between which the steer tears along, hightailing it for freedom. The dogging cowboy dives headlong off his flying horse onto the back of the running steer. Grabbing a solid hold on the long, spikey horns, the dogger is dragged as though fastened to a runaway train. Scrambling like mad, he stabs his boot heels into the ground, plowing a furrow deep enough to bury a body (possibly his own) in an effort to stop the lunging animal's forward race. Using the horns as handles, the bull dogger tries to twist off the critter's head, or at least far enough that the steer's body has to follow, flopping both man and beast to the ground with the steer's four feet pointed at the sky. If the critter falls on its side with its feet still grounded, the dogger must wrench its head around till the animal rolls over, forcing its feet skyward as it goes. In an instant the dogger leaps to his own feet and coolly stalks off as though out for a stroll. (Bull doggers learn their cool-stroll walk from watching old John Wayne movies.) Rarely does the cowboy deign to look back at the steer he's just jerked into the dust. Sometimes this is a mistake. Usually steers, unlike bulls, don't try to gore a man, but the occa-

sional exception to this rule can surprise a meandering dogger into a Flying Nun leap over the nearest fence. The
crowd applauds.

CALF ROPING: A comparatively tame event, roping
requires a great deal of skill on the part of both cowboy
and cowhorse. Calf roping can earn the contestant a nice
sum of money, and if he doesn't get stove up by falling off
a bucking bronc, he may be able to pay for the expense of
trailering his personal roping horse around the country
from rodeo to rodeo.

The roper, lariat shaken loose and held at ready, posi-
tions himself on his nervous quarter horse alongside a narrow chute usually at the far end of an arena. At a signal, a
calf is spooked out of the chute, and moments later, the
roper bursts through a string barrier and hurtles after it.
The calf is required to have a few seconds head start, and
should the rider break the barrier before the calf passes a
designated point, he is penalized five seconds off his time.
The roper thunders after the running calf, lariat whirling in
a sizzling loop as he attempts to drop it over the calf's
head. The quicker the animal is caught the better if the
roper wants to win money.

The moment the lasso settles around the calf, the
horse slams on its brakes and comes to a skidding halt,
while the rider dallies the rope around the saddle horn,
making a straight, taut line between caught calf and horse.
Without wasting a second, the cowboy piles off, lopes up
to the calf who is standing with the rope crushing his wind-
pipe and bawling. The cowboy reaches across the top of
the animal, grabs a front and a hind leg and attempts to
flip the critter on its side. This is sometimes successful, but
occasionally the calf has grown past baby-calf age clear on
to adolescence and outweighs the man trying to throw it
down.

Once the roper has the calf splatted on the ground, he then grabs his piggin' string. This has nothing to do with pigs. It is a short piece of thin rope that is carried looped through the roper's belt or stuck in a hindside pocket. Frantically, the cowboy gathers up three of the calf's feet, two hind ones and a front one usually, and drops the loop of his piggin' string around the bunched-together feet. Flipping the rope twice around the calf's feet, he loops it back in a half hitch, then leaps to his own feet and reaches for the sky as though about to lead a cheer. This gesture indicates he has finished tying. There follows a tense silence from the crowd while the calf struggles to loosen itself from the bonds. Another rider, holding aloft a small red signal flag, keeps a steady eye on the calf, too. After ten seconds, if the animal cannot free itself, the flag comes down, and the roper is still in the running for prize money. The next rider lines up his horse and commences to repeat the performance, but fortunately with a fresh calf.

Women ride in rodeos too, but most choose to stay off the broncs. They prefer to compete in goat-tying competitions, which are the same as calf roping, except the goats are lighter creatures, and women can lift them more easily. They also compete in Barrel Racing, an event where barrels are set up in a triad formation and the rider figure-eights her horse around the barrels and then races back to the starting line. This event, also run against the clock, requires a highly trained horse to make the tight turns and keep up the speed necessary to win. Like good roping horses, a good barrel horse can earn its owner a pot full of money.

Throughout the rodeo, which lasts for about three and a half hours, the crowd happily consumes enough beer to float every horse there. By afternoon's end, the standby ambulance has carted off two or three damaged contestants to the local hospital. The kids are playing hide and seek under the grandstand or rope-the-post behind the corrals, and lines form in front of outhouses and tall bushes.

EDIFYING WOOLLY WEST EDICTS

How does a would-be rodeo hand learn his trade?
Answer: Instantly.

• ● •

What does a rodeo cowboy win?
Answer: Money, broken bones, rest stops in hospitals and the besotted admiration of teenage girls and Greenhorn women.

CHAPTER 20

HOW TO BE A MIGHTY HUNTER
(Beware of anyone wearing orange and toting a gun)

Out West, hunting is a religion. If you feel the urge to join those legions of sporting persons, make sure what you're shooting at is actually legally targeted wild game.

Remember that horns grow on cows and bulls. Antlers grow on deer, moose and elk. Forget buffalo. They're protected on reservations to prevent final annihilation. Ascertain the difference between wild game and cows, steers, horses and the odd sheep that may amble by. To shoot any of these makes a rancher testy and may shorten your own life. If you cut a fence in order to gain access to hunting, no one will sympathize when you're found mysteriously shot.

To help persuade unknowledgeable hunters that a no trespassing, no hunting sign means what it says, the county pays its law officers and Fish and Game personnel to ride herd on hunters. Improperly taken animals, or shooting an animal not in this year's description of designated game, can net you fines, confiscation of your kill and sometimes a vacation in the local jail. Shoot a relative if you must, but do not shoot game out of season.

Probably one of the West's most entertaining sights is the fall influx of hunters straight from the big city. Driving enormous vehicles chock full of an unbelievable quantity of expensive gear and booze, booze, booze, they descend on the area like a cricket plague. It staggers the imagination to see a vehicle at dawn's early light piloted by a bunch of hung-over hunters carrying high-powered rifles they don't necessarily know how to handle.

During the months of hunting season, postpone riding the range. If you absolutely must ride, wear bright orange clothing, and over your horse's rump hang a fat double sign reading, "Horse. Do Not Shoot." On your own back, hang another sign that declares, "Person Riding a Horse. Do Not Shoot." Last year, three people got their signs punctuated. To be entirely safe, the cautious soul will ride the range inside an armoured car.

Once you've sent the spirit of that moose, deer, elk,

antelope, mountain sheep or goat to its heavenly home, what do you do with the rest of it?

Assuming you have managed to drag the creature out of whatever wilds you shot it in, the animal must then be disassembled and processed into edible chops, steaks, roasts and stew meat. This involves saws, knives and blood. You must skin your catch, gut it, get rid of the unpleasant bowels and other interior organs, hang the carcass for awhile, take it down, cut it up, wrap the pieces in butcher paper and put them into a freezer somewhere. If your freezer is only the upper compartment of your fridge and presently holds ice trays and three pizzas, you may be obliged to rent a freezer locker from the meat processing plant in town—or in some town reasonably near where you reside.

If you have no stomach for meat-cutting in your own kitchen, you may haul the entire dead animal to the meat packing plant in the first place. For a fee, they will do all the nasty part and even put the wrapped meat in a locker for you. After that, it's a matter of bragging about the wild meat you personally bagged, inviting friends to dinner, giving away deer, antelope or moose burger to the needy, and keeping the dogs healthy with stew-bones and liver. Supplemental wild meat is a noble, necessary and even tasty facet of Western life, especially if someone else cooks it.

EDIFYING WOOLLY WEST EDICTS

What is the penalty for shooting game out of season?
Answer: One to five years, courtesy of the State Pen.

• ● •

What is the penalty for shooting a philandering spouse out of season?
Answer: One to five years, suspended.

PART V

WOOLLY WEST COMMUNITY ACTIVITIES

WHAT TO DO IN THE WILDERNESS

CHAPTER 21

WOOLLY WEST
CULTURAL ENTERPRISES
*(Join something. You'll become an officer
right away. This is not flattery.)*

Greenhorns may experience qualms about lack of cultural opportunities in the Woolly West. Fear not. Small towns and rural areas can happily involve even the least assertive person in clubs and organizations. You can choose to garden or grow flowers, sew or spin, do crafts, pistol shoot, attend regular business meetings, shape the town's destiny at Chamber of Commerce meetings, talk up at Toastmasters, play bridge, ski, ride with the Saddle Club, bowl, exchange recipes at Woman's Club and join an assortment of musical groups . . . to name only a few gregarities.

Each organization meets at certain times and places during the week or month and will rigidly guard its particular scheduling, as divinely ordained.

Should you join any team activity such as Bridge Club, remember that showing up on Club night becomes a sacred obligation. Nothing takes priority over Bridge. If you're pregnant, schedule delivery before, after, but never on, the same night as Bridge Club. If the President or First Lady calls, get the number and say you'll call back later.

When one capricious woman failed to appear at the expected time, the Bridge Club hostess alerted the Sheriff, the Deputies and the Posse. They scoured the town, located the missing player and gave her a siren-blowing escort to that evening's game.

You can be honorably absent only if you produce a substitute to fill your slot. Any warm body will do. The person need have only minimal playing skill as the group always makes the sub the dummy during each hand anyway.

In Woolly West communities, people who like horses form a Saddle Club. Throughout the summer, members gallop about on their steeds at the local fairgrounds, breathing and eating dust thick enough to butter. They compete in relay races, barrel races, team competitions, goat-tying and other assorted sweaty pursuits. There's something ultimately satisfying about a day spent with your horse, especially if he carries you to victory in the potato race.

Saddle Clubbers also gather with their horses to "go on a trail ride." A trail ride may be a few hours or a few days. Beginning early in the morning, riders meander over hill and dale eventually stopping at a pre-chosen site where they dismount, share lunches packed in saddlebags, apply Corona to galled places on their mounts and themselves, take a nap, climb back in the saddle and ride home again, totally happy in spite of blisters, mosquitoes, saddle-sores, heel flies and throbbing knee joints.

Community Chorus is a less physically active organization composed of town and country folk who like to sing. The chorus presents a Christmas program, an Easter program, a summer program performed during Pioneer Day in the park, and matinee performances at the local Rest Home. Both general and Rest Home audiences appreciate chorus efforts as every member is somebody's close relative. During the finale number, tambourines are passed around, and the entire audience joins in the singing and thumping.

Those who prefer to beat, blow, bang, thump, whistle, tinkle or toot as musical expression, can join the Community Band. Anyone may join the band. Musical background or ability have no bearing on qualifying. Beginners whose sense of rhythm isn't good enough to play a regular instrument, will be assigned to the percussion section.

In addition to the occasional public performance, the band may also decide to march in the annual, Rodeo Parade . . . always a gratifying experience. During one memorable parade, a fledgling bass-drummer, marching with vigor and bopping with abandon, fell upon misfortune. The drum-harness slipped, the big boomer dropped to the pavement, rolled a ways and turtled over on its side in the middle of the street. The rest of the band played on, leaving the drumless marcher defenseless before the oncoming Black-Horse Sheriff's Posse, parading behind the band. Stepping haughtily, two by two, the horses tried to avoid the hapless, struggling leftover musician. One skittish animal snorted, shied sideways, reared and danced on its hind legs. Then the spooked black dropped to all fours, bashing a hoof through the drumhead, an action that instantly threw him into a frenzy. The frightened creature began rearing and bucking, trying to rid itself of its oversized ankle bracelet. On the third jump, Black Beauty shook off his drum and his rider, who bounced twice before scrambling to his feet. Aiming a vicious kick at the fallen drum, the unhorsed posseman limped after his escaping cayuse, while the embarrassed drummer, collecting his shattered instrument, ran to beat the band, too.

Regardless of the activity focus of organizations, all of them, in order to earn funds, hold bake sales luncheons, or sell pie and coffee at various functions. Everyone has the privilege of sweating in the kitchen to produce items that will be sold at less than cost. While it may seem circular financing, it's against small town rules to donate simple money or anything storebought. Sara Lee has no place at a genuine bake sale.

Failure to bake a donation for your club is inexcusable. Should you be absent because you're traveling in Europe, bake ahead. If you break a leg, start your contribution earlier in the day so you can hobble along to the sale place in plenty of time. If you suffer a death in the family, you must still create an offering, unless the death is yours. Even then, it's advisable to have something in readiness in the freezer.

In conjunction with the annual Flower Show, the Garden Club chooses to sell pie and coffee to make money. Naturally, dedicated members stay up nights cooking. The flower exhibit is outstanding. Held in a roomy auditorium, banks of bright blooms are ranged on sheet-covered tables and stair-stepped risers. Committee women work from first light cataloging, judging and placing artistically arranged floral creations in vases, in baskets, in unusual holders such as rusty old coffee pots, on rustic branches, on weathered boards, in crystal bowls.

Upon entering the auditorium, a symphony of color and fragrance softly saturates your senses. After viewing every arrangement and bouquet, inhaling every scent and comparing each award winner, it's time to buy pie. Purchase a piece of your favorite and sit down at one of the cloth-covered tables, centerpieced with cut-glass vases, each holding a single fragrant posey.

This is a good time to chat with other women. It is at the Flower Show where you may first meet Mrs. Ursula Pipsworthing. She will be holding court in a pale-peach slack suit at an adjacent table. Aim for a good impression upon Mrs. P. as she is a member of the town's social elite. In fact, she is its only member. Repartee pleasantly, chat graciously and move cautiously. Heed the sad lesson learned by one newcomer. Intent on making a good impression, she resisted a second piece of pie, rose with dignity and bade Mrs. Pipsworthing goodbye. Picking up her handbag, she swept smoothly away, unfortunately snagging the tablecloth as she swept, causing bud-vase and flower to soar in a graceful swan-dive into Mrs. P.'s lap, where they lay, dripping. The poor Greenhorn has never returned to really comfortable repartee terms with Mrs. Pipsworthing.

EDIFYING WOOLLY WEST EDICTS

What do newcomers find abounding in Woolly West towns?

Answer: Quaintness and charm.

• ● •

What do newcomers want to do with these attributes?

Answer: Have them bronzed.

CHAPTER 22

TRUE GRIT
(Courage, Camille)

In small towns Out West, horseback riding is available to all. Even those who don't actually live on a ranch can own a horse, join the Saddle Club and participate in trail rides, horse shows and gymkhanas. Gymkhanas or O-Mok-Sees are competitive games on horseback. During my first summer in the Woolly West, I acquired Smokey, the loveliest equine ever born, who carried me to victory on many occasions.

It was during one such horsey competition that I learned about true grit. Frances and I were standing alongside our steeds on the grassy area outside the fairgrounds arena where a gymkhana was in progress. We had paired up during the team competitions, coming in second in the Back-to-Back Doubles Race, wherein one person (me) rode backwards while the other person (Frances) steered the head end.

Our team had won first in the Bucket Relay Race where we were required to pass a plastic container full of water from one rider to another while going full gallop around the track. I was having the time of my life. I rode in the potato, the barrel and the quarter-mile race. I had proven myself capable of anything, I thought. Nothing could shake my confidence on this perfect summer day.

It was then Frances said, "The Shovel Race is next."

"Shovel Race? What's a Shovel Race?" I asked.

She explained that one person would ride bareback while another person would ride a scoop shovel hitched on behind the horse. The teams would race one at a time against the clock.

"Saddles aren't allowed in this race," said Frances, "and since I'm a better bareback rider than you, I'll let you ride the shovel."

As we talked, she busily hitched a shiny aluminum scoop shovel to the south end of her tall, sorrel horse, Doodle. Leather tug lines led from a horsecollar, crossed over Doodle's rump, looped through the shovel handle and then splayed out to fasten to rings on either end of a singletree lashed crosswise to the base of the shovel. (A singletree has nothing to do with trees.)

A smidgin of trepidation stirred in my depths. I wasn't enchanted with the prospect of placing my body on that shovel.

"Here," said Frances, handing over Doodle's reins, "you bring my horse while I go get us a contestant number."

She took off, leaving me to find my way to the arena entrance. Bunched around the arena gate was a passel of kids, goats, chickens, cats, dogs, two frisky colts, several frogs tethered with fishing line, some lambs and a bowl of goldfish. The motley assemblage was awaiting the start of the Pet Parade scheduled after the Shovel Race. One ingenious child had a pet pig outfitted in a dog harness with the end of the lead rope looped through his belt, leaving both his hands free to hold a handsome rainbow-feathered Banty rooster.

Opening the clumsy arena gate, I led Doodle through, closed the gate, and warned the kids to be sure to keep it **shut** during the ensuing Shovel Race.

Doodle pranced happily, his paprika hide gleaming, the posies Frances had stuck in his collar bobbing merrily.

Frances appeared waving two oilcloth squares, each bearing the number 14. Lordy, I thought. I was going to have to wait around watching 13 other contestants bite the dust. I started feeling nervous.

Safety-pinning an oilcloth square on the back of my new pink western shirt, Frances pointed out that the waiting time could be well spent observing other shovel-riders' techniques.

The starting flag snapped down and the first pair of contestants blasted off. The scoop shovel and its jockey, a wild-eyed yipping kid, swathed through loose turf, dirt spraying from each side like the wake behind a boat. At the south end of the arena near the gate I had carefully closed, the horse zoomed into a U-turn, and the kid flipped off his shovel like a pebble shot from a sling. He rolled over and over, collecting an overcoat of dust. I bowed my head on

Doodle's rump, trying to hide my growing unease.

"Be sure to hang on," Frances admonished. "That last rider should never have let go."

I could see that hanging on sure was the key factor. Each rider in turn departed his shovel in a new and innovative manner. All gathered the same thick dust.

All too soon my number came up. Frances steadied Doodle while I gingerly lowered my posterior onto the scoop, frogbent my legs, braced my feet on the singletree crosspiece, doubled my torso forward and grasped the shovel handle with a white-knuckled overlapping grip. The view before me was less than inspiring. Taking a deep breath, I vowed nothing was going to dislodge me. For insurance, I offered a fervent prayer. I inhaled. I exhaled. I concentrated.

Frances leaned over me, her voice solemn, her expression grimly serious. "I'm counting on you. If we can win this race, we have more points than anybody here." She placed a hand on my shoulder and patted it. "You can do it. You've got true grit," she said.

I decided to die before letting go of that darned shovel handle. Frances leaped aboard Doodle and nudged him to the starting point. In the stands, the watching crowd tensed, sensing drama. The flag cracked. Frances' heels thunked into Doodle's flanks, and we were off. I squinted as the horse's pounding hooves sent clods of what I hoped was dirt, flying into my face. The spongy turf became a painful jarring washboard. Hunching lower, I thrust my head forward, vulturelike, my entire being pouring energy into clenching my fingers around the wooden handle. Approaching the U-turn, I was horrified to see that the arena gate stood open! Closing my eys, I resorted to prayer. It was all I had.

Suddenly the jolting, heaving ride became a bone-bruising battering as Doodle shot out through the wide-open gate. Terror rode my scoop. I heard yells and screams, many of them mine. Opening one eye, I perceived a mixed herd of kids and animals. Frances hollered, "LOOK OUT!" She also hollered other words I was surprised she knew.

Hauling mightily on the reins, she tried to turn Doodle. We were going faster than a speeding bullet when the shovel tipped. Somehow, as the left side of my formerly pink shirt sledded across the terrain, I maintained a grip on that shovel handle while my body stayed frozen in its frog-bent position.

"HANG IN THERE," howled Frances. "We're going back through the gate! Don't let go!"

I clamped shut my eyes, feeling safer in the dark. As Doodle galloped past the melee of kids and animals crowded at the gate, something slammed into my chest, and a hideous screech blasted my eardrums. Slitting open my eyes, I stared eyeball to eyeball at a Banty rooster. Nothing tastes worse than chicken with the feathers still on.

Somehow I remained laminated to the scoop shovel like a tick on a sheep, while a terrified rooster screeched in my ear and beat his wings on my person. Then the swirling, bucking scoop banged into a gate post. The blow jolted the feathered hitch-hiker from the shelter of my bosom and jarred my feet off the singletree. My body unfurled from its froggy posture, but my hands increased their death grip on the handle. Like a flag in a stiff breeze, me and my scoop whipped and flailed as Doodle thundered the length of the arena. I knew not when we crossed the finish line. I only knew my flight had slowed. I sprawled full length, like a stretched-out noodle. But I had not let go that handle! My burning hands were welded to its hardwood surface.

Somewhere a voice called. Someone asked if I were all right. Slowly I opened my eyes. The chicken was gone. The scenery had quit hurtling past. "Is it over?" I whispered.

"Congratulations," said Frances. "You did just great! You can let go, now," she added.

Let go? Lying there in the turf, my cheek mashed against the tilted handle, I was convinced I would never move again. Sadly I contemplated spending the rest of my life with a shovel welded between my palms.

Then I heard a Commanche yelp, and Frances bent over me, a victorious smile lighting her countenance. "We won! WE WON!" she shouted. Then, like peeling a banana, she began unlacing my fingers. I sat there in the dust among the horse cookies with my palms threatening to ignite and felt a surge of happiness. I had learned the meaning of True Grit.

EDIFYING THE WOOLLY WEST EDICTS

As a tenderfoot Out West, is it mandatory that you ride horses and love cows?

Answer: Not necessarily, but . . . keep it a secret.

— ● —

CHAPTER 23

THE PLAY'S THE THING
(Or: Rose Was A Good Old Soul)

Newcomers seeking a hobby, entertainment or creative outlet beyond rodeos, barn dances and knitting clubs can get involved in the Little Theater Group. Small town Thespians make up in enthusiasm what they perhaps lack in professional sophistication. (Mention "summer stock" to a Westerner, and he will think you mean cows grazing.)

Frances, a ham of not fully plumbed depths, invited me to participate in the production of that famous drama, "Good Old Soul." The plot centered around Lady Bentwhistle who became distressed about the plight of her affianced, Lord Bertram Piltdown who had got himself in a pickle in deepest Africa and, along with old Rose, her maid, sought to extricate Lord Piltdown from his pickle. Frances accepted the lead role of Lady B., but I, as a modest shy beginner and a Greenhorn, merely volunteered to be the stage-manager's helper.

On opening night, two hours before curtain time, Frances informed me that the woman playing Old Rose had gone down with the flu.

"She can't do her part," said Frances.

I was aghast, knowing that Lady Bentwhistle's maid was an important supporting character. "We can't get along without Rose," I sympathized.

Frances pounced. "I know," she said. "You'll have to take the part."

Horrified, I argued I couldn't possibly learn the lines in the short time till curtain.

Frances was adamant. "Mostly all Rose says is, 'no, Mum, yes, Mum' and curtsies whenever Lady Bentwhistle addresses her. You've helped stage-manage all through rehearsals. The lines will come to you." She paused. "You don't want to let down the whole community do you?"

I succumbed. How could I fail my new hometown?

An hour later, as the curtain lifted, I found myself standing in the wings awaiting my cue—the bing-bong chime of a doorbell. Lady Bentwhistle would then say, "Hark," and I, as Old Rose, would enter. Nervously I adjusted my costume. With my hair sprayed silver and skinned into a tight bun, my head resembled a peeled onion. Atop my onion cranium perched a puff-ball maid's cap. The original Rose, I had discovered, was a foot taller than I, so I had accommodated by blousing the long black skirt over the waistband of my floor-length white work apron. I prayed I'd get through the evening.

"If you get stuck for words," Frances advised, "just think of a logical response a maid would make and ad lib."

With my brain functioning about as fast as a soggy sponge, I didn't believe I could possibly ad lib anything. Lady Bentwhistle, her hair a mass of sausage curls, her bustled Victorian gown dripping lace, was just finishing a dramatic soliloquy. With one hand to delicate brow, she bemoaned the fate of her affianced, Sir Bertram Piltdown, gone off on safari into Africa, where he searched for the whereabouts of the fierce Umgoomba Tribe. Lord Piltdown aimed to snitch the Sacred Golden Ingot, a Cyclops adornment imbedded in the brow of Goomba, the deity worshipped by the Umgoomba people.

I listened to Frances emoting. "Oh, Bertie, Bertie. It has been weeks, my love, since you've left my side to search for the Sacred Golden Ingot. I fear," (here, Frances brought a lace hanky to her lips and stifled a sob), "I fear for your safety, dear Bertie."

"Bing-bong," went a chime. There was a pause. "Hark, someone comes," said Lady B., cupping her hand to her ear. Another pause. Frances held her pose, lifted her brows and looked expectant. Gosh, I thought watching her eyes roll, she can really act.

Moving her cupped hand from ear to mouth, Lady Bentwhistle raised her voice. "Rose, Rose!," she called. "Come at once. I need you!" I jumped. Oh my gosh, I was supposed to have entered when Frances harked!

Like Jack popping out of the box, I bounded on stage and spring-boarded over to Frances. "Yes, Mum!" I curtseyed.

"The door, Rose," said Lady Bentwhistle.

"Yes, Mum?" I repeated stupidly. I could hear titters from beyond the footlights. I broke out in a sweat, and an awful pinging started in my ears. Stiffly I moved to a doorway downstage, opened it, glanced down and saw a shoebox-sized parcel wrapped in brown paper. I forgot what I was supposed to do, so I just kept looking down.

"Bring what you find over **here,** Rose," Lady B. called. There was an edge in her voice.

"Yes, Mum," I muttered, scooped up the package and wheeled. My foot, catching in the hem of my draggy costume, catapaulted me forward, smack into Lady Bentwhistle. The momentum carried us both onto a Victorian sofa, and the parcel flew off stage into the first row of audience where it settled on a fat man's stomach.

The crowd broke into laughter. I was so embarrassed, I decided simply to remain where I was and die, but Frances never lost her cool. Rising quickly, she cuffed me to my feet. "Don't be clumsy, Rose," then extending her lace-covered arm, she pointed an imperious finger and in a marvelously modulated British accent, commanded, "Fetch me yon pahcel, Rose. There's a good old soul."

I dipped another curtsy. "Yes, Mum," I said, scuttling to the edge of the stage where the chubby fellow kindly handed me back the shoebox.

"Open the pahcel, Rose, I implore you," ordered Lady Bentwhistle, flopping her sausage curls. "I fear it may be a message from Lord Piltdown."

"Yes, Mum." Ripping off the brown wrapping. I peered inside the box. There was a pause.

"Well, what IS it, Rose," asked Lady Bentwhistle, her patience clearly being tested.

"Er," I said, ad-libbing cleverly, "looks like a doorknob."

Desperately Frances corrected me. "I believe you have an ingot there, Rose. And surely, there's a note—at the bottom of the pahcel?"

I peeked under the knob. "Sure is," I answered proudly. "And here it is!" I waved a paper.

The audience cheered. Startled, I grinned across the footlights. This acting was heady stuff.

Frances, grabbing the note, milked dramatic mileage out of reading it. "My Dearest," she intoned, "find a safe place for the enclosed bauble. I shall join you soon. Your bethrothed, Bertie."

The plot thickened when Lady Bentwhistle's happiness grew cloudy as she learned that Lord Piltdown had fallen into the hands of the fierce Umgoombas. She determined that she and of course, her maid, old Rose, would journey to Africa to find him.

Scene II found us struggling through a hot, steamy,

varmint-infested jungle constructed of cardboard, paper-mache and sagebruch stuck in buckets. Rope snakes, rubber bugs and tobacco-wire spiders dropped or flew about as we beat our way through the foliage.

Frances' costume had changed to a long-skirted khaki safari garment. She carried a riding crop in one hand and a hanky in the other. Atop her springy curls, a pith helmet squatted like a mushroom.

My costume remained the same, except for the addition of a similar mushroom helmet that kept slipping over my eyes. Naturally, good old Rose carried the precious ingot tied to my waist in a cloth bag that sagged to my shins. The darned ingot keep bonking my kneecaps.

"Ohhhh," moaned Lady Bentwhistle, flicking her crop at a bug, "we are lost in this wretched jungle." As she sank pathetically to the jungle floor, exhausted, her pith helmet fell off and caromed across the stage, jumping the footlights. The, by now, alert fat man, tossed it back, and it rolled in a wide curve, finally wobbling to rest at Frances' feet.

"We shall die, I fear," groaned Frances, "lost in the jungle, far from home and kin."

"Yes, Mum," I said, staggering and lurching about before piling up on the floor next to Frances.

"Ohhhh, would that I could clap eyes on dearest Bertie Piltdown just once again," wailed Lady B. "Ohhhh, Bertie, Bertie."

Just then, a deep rolling male voice offstage groaned wretchedly. "Ohhhh, that my cruel captors would but put me out of my hideous misery. Ohhhh, would that I could clap eyes on my beloved Philomena Bentwhistle before I expire. Ohhhh, Philly, Philly . . ."

At this point, naturally, Lady B. sent good old Rose to investigate the piteous moaning, which meant I had to crawl on hands and knees while peering from under my pith helmet through a bunch of snake-draped sagebrush.

In the final act, the curtain opened to reveal Lord Piltdown, played by the Reverend Barrymore Hibbs, tied to a stake. Bearing a remarkable resemblance to Mickey Rooney, Rev. Hibbs wore a pith helmet, a monocle, a raggedy torn khaki shirt and jungle shorts that ended just above knobby knees. Hibbs' legs were so bowed he looked like a walking set of parentheses. Near Lord Piltdown loomed a huge seated figure of the god, Goomba, constructed of paper-mache over a wooden two-by-four scaffolding and mounted on a platform five feet off the floor. The diety's generous stomach sagged and its arms stretched invitingly over a cauldron (a child's camouflaged wading pool) filled with boiling goat oil. (Dry ice, hidden from view, made spirals of steam.) Half a dozen fierce Umgoomba natives in BVDs, leather loin cloths, beads and feathers, self-consciously stirred the goat oil with broomstick spears. Poor Lord P. was scheduled to become meat in a jungle stew because he had filched the sacred Ingot.

Reverend Hibbs struggled with his bonds. Deepening his voice, he emoted, "The Ingot . . . only the return of the sacred Ingot can save me."

"Hang in there," yelled the fat man.

Hidden behind bushes, Lady Bentwhistle and her hapless maid trembled. Then Lady B. stagewhispered, "Rose, take the sacred Ingot and replace it in Goomba's forehead."

"Yes, Mum," I whispered. Firming my jaw, I crept forward, knees catching on my long skirt, the Ingot in its bag, clonking on the stage floor as I dragged along. Finally, in desperation, Rose lurched to her feet. Murmuring, "Yes, Mum," again, I bloused the excess skirt material over my apron waistband.

"Atta girl, Rose!" shouted the fat fellow, whom I now viewed as a personal friend.

Tension built as Lord P. squirmed at the stake, Lady B. peered from behind her bush, and the natives, one of whom had forgotten to remove his Timex, muttered invectives as they stirred boiling oil.

Stealthily, I tippy-toed behind Goomba and began climbing his rear scaffolding. The audience cheered when I reached his neck. Clinging with one hand, I slithered the other arm around his broad face, feeling for the hole in his brow. I could barely reach it.

Below me, the natives removed Lord Piltdown from the stake and shoved him toward the steaming cauldron.

"Oh, no!" shrieked Lady Bentwhistle. Her unfortunate outburst led to her discovery and capture. Now the natives had two for tea. Lord Piltdown and Lady Bentwhistle strained toward each other, emotion twisting their features. Lady B.'s curls boinged. "Bertie," she moaned. Lord P.'s monocle fell off. "Philly," he croaked.

The audience cheered again as I poked my head into view from behind Goomba's skull. Reaching around, I shoved the doorknob into the Cyclops hole just as Lady Bentwhistle called, "Look, look! The Sacred Ingot has been returned!"

For a moment the stage darkened and a spotlight beaconed in on Goomba's brow.

"Umgow-w-w-waaaaaa," sighed the natives. Dropping spears and captives, they fell to their knees, touching foreheads to floor. "Umgow-wa-wa-wa-aaaaaa," they repeated.

"Good going, Rose, old girl," called Lady Bentwhistle.

"Yes, Mum," I said and made the mistake of curtseying. My foot skidded off the narrow scaffolding. Pitching forward, I grabbed Goomba around his thick neck which swung me around to the fore where I clung, lip to lip for several seconds, my feet dangling above the goat oil. My pith helmet fell into the oil. Then my sweaty palms slipped, and I too, dropped like a shot, crumpling on the bottom of the vat.

Shaken, but unhurt, I made my way groggily to the edge of the cauldron, kilroyed my nose over the rim and peeked out. I saw Lady Bentwhistle and Lord Piltdown gazing soulfully at each other while waiting for the hysterically laughing audience to simmer down. I realized the laughter was aimed at me. Lordy, how was I going to ad-lib out of this? Moments passed. The audience wouldn't stop laughing. I could see my friend, the fat man, his tummy shaking and quivering. Finally, Frances, rising once again to the occasion, moved to the cauldron, placed her hand on my head and mashed old Rose out of sight.

"Poor Rose," said Lady Bentwhistle sadly, "she was a good old soul."

The curtains closed.

EDIFYING WOOLLY WEST EDICTS

Who attends a small town dramatic production?
Answer: The entire populace.

• ● •

When does the audience arrive?
Answer: At least an hour before curtain time.

• ● •

Who sits in the front rows?
Answer: Grandmothers and grandfathers.

• ● •

Who sits on the floor in front of the stage?
Answer: Grandchildren.

CHAPTER 24

WOOLLY WEST DUDE RANCHING
*(Dude horses and dude wranglers
can withstand nearly anything)*

Because of my experience as a dude-ranch employee one summer, I have never since had to resort to soap operas to obtain a slice of life.

Dude ranches abound in the Woolly West. Easterners, used to comforts, attention and plush surroundings, journey Out West to these havens of rustic ruggedness in order to live in freezing cabins without indoor bathrooms, eat plain food, blister themselves in odd spots riding horses and listen to ranch hands tell tall tales.

As a newcomer to the Wild West, I earned my keep as an employee on a "working dude ranch." On a working ranch, the guests help trail the beef cattle to summer pasture and learn how to pull faucets on the Jersey milk cow, a remarkably unflappable bovine. Guests live in rustic log cabins with wood-burning stoves for heat and no indoor plumbing. Employees live in clapboard cabins with wood-burning stoves and also no indoor plumbing.

Dude ranching tends to be sexist and macho. Male employees wrangle horses and dudes. Female employees wrangle cooking, serving and cleaning. Cowboys take guests on trail rides, flirt with the women dudes, tell tall cowboy stories and participate in the five o'clock cocktail hour. Women employees wash dishes, make beds, cook meals and serve the hors d'oeuvres at the five o'clock cocktail hour.

THE COWBOY AND THE LADY

He was called Brick because of his thick thatch of carroty hair. He was also tall, with a cleft chin. He wrangled horses for the ranch. He wrangled women for himself.

Her name was Ella. A plain name, but it suited her. She was average tall with glasses and a timid smile. Ella was a secretary from Chicago. All year she hoarded money so she could come as a guest in the summer to the ranch where Brick wrangled horses and women.

Passion developed. This was not a surprise to Brick.

Behind her glasses, Ella's eyes glittered whenever Brick moseyed near. Most every afternoon, Brick would saddle two horses, and he and Ella would ride the trail until they found a spot perfect for nature study. For two weeks, Ella spent the happiest hours of her slipping-fast young womanhood studying bounteous nature among the sage bushes.

Then one afternoon, Ella and Brick returned early. Brick rode kind of funny, almost side saddle and hunched over. Ella looked downcast. She took her evening meal in her room. Brick took his in the bunk house.

As an employee, I thoughtfully fetched a tray of food to Ella's room. It was only natural we got to talking. I could see the poor woman was pent up. My expressed sympathy unpent her. Gradually the story emerged. It seemed that Ella and Brick had ridden up Timber Draw to a favorite spot near a babbling brook. Taking shade beneath a single old cottonwood tree, they fell to inflaming one another. Meanwhile, the horses stood by lazily flicking their tails and occasionally stamping a foot to dislodge a pesky heel fly. Ground tied, the horses grazed peacefully for awhile, but as horses are wont to do, they too, decided to shade up beneath the cottonwood.

Brick and Ella paid no mind. After all there was plenty of room beneath the tree, although concern about sharing shade with the horses was not foremost in Brick or Ella's thoughts. Perhaps it should have been. As Ella and Brick lay relaxing side by side, facing one another, discussing nature's beauty, a heel fly sank its fangs into Brick's horse. Startled, the animal jumped forward straight toward Brick and Ella. Now, horses instinctively avoid stepping on a person, and Brick's horse was no exception. A sharp hoof cleavered the ground neatly between Ella and Brick, avoiding all of Ella—and almost all of Brick.

SOFIE'S PRIME

Sofie, a small person, chirpy as a wren, confided she was 69. I suspected she had been 69 and holding for a good long time, but Sofie considered her prime as still to be reached. Each afternoon, one of my duties was to knock at her door to remind her that Happy Hour was approaching. She needed the advance warning to give her time to apply pounds of makeup, gallons of perfume and three-inch false eyelashes. The lashes may have interfered with vision, but seeing clearly was not a priority with Sofie.

She had achieved outstanding excellence in the art of

making an entrance into any social gathering. Always dressed in something long and diaphanous for Happy Hour, she would glide into the ranch parlor, one arm lifted as though about to bestow a benediction. Dropping anchor near a convenient table or high-backed chair, she would assume a Mae West pose, head tilted so she could flirtatiously glance up through her lashes. Scarcely five-feet tall in heels, she could look up at everyone, but reserved her most appealing flickers for the men, who sooner or later, drifted with the current to her side. When the dinner gong sounded, she butterflyed between two escorts into the dining room.

One afternoon, my knock on Sofie's door went unanswered. A little worried, I opened the door. From the bathroom came strange gurgling noises.

"Sofie?" I called.

A figure dressed in a brilliant, peacock-blue satin dressing gown came stumbling from the bathroom. For a moment, I was startled until I realized the blue thing under her chin was not a wound, but a satin chin strap.

With crimson varnish-tipped nails, a fluttering hand indicated her throat, from which issued turkey gobbles along with bubbles that floated free in the air where afternoon sunbeams brushed in tiny rainbows. Sputtering, Sofie spun around and disappeared into the bathroom. Concerned she might be having a seizure, I followed, trying to recall whether one applied mouth to mouth or the Heimlich Maneuver for this type of malady. Sofie was bent over the sink, rinsing her mouth again and again. Finally she could speak. Pointing to a flask-shaped shampoo bottle, she gasped, "I thought it was Scotch!"

THE EQUESTRIENNE

Sofie loved riding. During her stay at the ranch, she always asked for Dandy, a gentle horse, one that could be counted on not to strain himself past a walk. Although she joined in every group trail ride, Sofie also loved riding alone. One afternoon, she rode off on Dandy. When she had not returned by five o'clock, we grew worried. Sofie would never intentionally miss Happy Hour. Especially concerned was Blinker Bill (a soubriquet earned because of the tendency of his left eye to blink constantly). Blinker Bill, who held his age nearly as well as Sofie did, saddled a horse and set out to find her. Sometime later, Bill returned accompanied by the lost Sofie. He looked a mite frazzled, but her smile could only be described as Cheshirelike.

As I helped her get ready for dinner, I asked, "Sofie, if you weren't lost, how come you stayed away so long?"

"Cowboys," answered Sofie innocently, "are such lonely men."

"Sofie! You don't mean . . . you . . . and old Blinker Bill . . . ? At your age?"

Old Sofie struck a hip-swiveling Mae West pose, flickered her lashes and declared, "Age, Dearie, has nothing to do with it."

JUST DESSERTS

While most dude-ranch guests are cheerful, pleasant people eager to enjoy their Woolly West vacations, some behave like mean plantation owners oppressing slaves. Employees, unable to please these martinets, have been known to resort to subterfuges and the occasional out and out prevarication.

Hazel Hurdurt, a New York entrepreneur (she said), was a medium tall, thin-lipped woman. She held her head on a slant as though leaning away from the prevailing wind. With her tan hair upswept on one side only, her skull appeared screwed on off center.

Hazel Hurdurt endeared herself to the ranch personnel from the first moment she stepped out of a chauffered limousine. "You may go, my good man," she said to the driver. She called all men, "my good man," and addressed all women with "there's a good girl."

Hazel felt it a matter of noblesse oblige to supervise and correct the behavior of us ranch vassals, including the ranch owner. From mystic heights, she issued orders. There was no escaping her. Tirelessly active, Hazel intended to experience fully every single aspect of Western living—but in her own style. While others wore jeans and boots, Hazel appeared in designer jodphurs and affected a foot-long cigarette holder that she waved a lot. The horse wrangler feared she would scare the horses or set the barn on fire.

We vassals became so fed up, we complained to the ranch owner. He didn't like her either, but reminded us that he had to suffer through dinner with her every evening. "Put up with her," he pleaded. "There's a bonus for everyone after she leaves. I'm charging her extra."

One evening, Hazel gave a private party to a select few in the small dining room. The employees' duties were simple. Prepare the food, withstand Hazel's haranguing and keep our mouths shut. On the morning of the occasion, several of us were busy baking, chopping, roasting and creating thousands of artful hors d'oeuvres and desserts. I had just finished laying out three-dozen lemon cookies on cooling racks when Hazel followed her cigarette holder into the kitchen.

"Put a lemon topping on those cookies," she commanded, peering slantwise down her nose. "Roll the rum balls in powdered sugar. Be sure to sprinkle coconut on the olive cream-cheese whorls, and don't forget to place a maraschino cherry on the cupcakes."

With enormous self control I refrained from telling Hazel where she could place her maraschinos. We laid the appetizers and desserts on utility trays and covered them with waxed paper and dampened tea towels. Hazel said that was the only way to keep them fresh.

When the party started, my job was to fetch in the appetizers. I lined up some imitation-crystal serving platters on the counter. Then I lifted the tea towel on the first tray of hors d'oeuvres. A black string lay across the tray of rum balls. Without my touching it, the string moved. And flowed. I stared at a column of black ants busily toting away bits of rum ball.

"Son-of-a-gun," I murmured and lifted the tea towel off the next tray. Among the coconut-olive cream cheese whorls, ants played tic-tac-toe as they carted off coconut sprinkles, a sprinkle at a time.

I thought of Hazel and smiled. I thought of a vanished bonus, possibly a vanished job. I looked at the clock. For the next few moments my fingers flew as I lifted each individual tidbit and blew, brushed, and flicked before placing it—mostly de-anted—on the crystal platter. I noticed some of the little buggers had gotten their tiny feet mired in the cheese whorls. Since I couldn't extract them, I spread more softened cheese on top.

Hazel's guests devoured the appetizers. One woman commented on the delicious subtle flavor of the coconut-olive cream-cheese whorls. "What," she asked, "are those delicious little black specks?"

"Protein bits," I answered. "Hazel suggested it."

EDIFYING WOOLLY WEST EDICTS

How do you tell a Dude from a normal Westerner?

Answer: The Dude drives a dirt-free car, wears matching color-coordinated clothing, sunglasses **and** a cowboy hat and never knows what to do with his time.

CHAPTER 25

THE FOURTH ESTATE IN THE WOOLLY WEST
(Hot off the grapevine)

Newspapering Out West remains a languid pursuit of the ordinary. Usually a weak, weekly effort, the local paper is subscribed to by every soul in the county and their relatives, in order to keep up with what went on a while back.

Though each issue totals a mere four to eight pages, the paper compensates for its slim bulk with an imposing name such as: "The Herald Tribune Clarion Independent Weekly Express Review." Within its pages, international news is ignored, national news is ignored and most state news is ignored. Occasionally current local news makes it to the printed page if someone bothers to phone in the pertinent information.

What is included in the weekly tabloid are births, deaths, marriages, divorces, graduations, high-school sports events, 4-H Club events, who visited whom over a holiday or weekend, classified announcements of ranch-hands wanted, library hours, rummage sales and bull auctions. A full-page spread, with pictures, appears immediately when the editor's daughter portrays a tree in the grade-school production of Hansel and Gretel, but reporting on the flood that wiped out county roads, washed away three barns and drowned a mule has to wait till next week.

Periodically, a local controversy over an issue such as a leash law to control wandering dogs can split a town, pit neighbors and friends against one another and cause a near endless rash of letters-to-the-editor. The town council goes into extra session to decide what to do.

People who loathe dogs favor a law requiring that canines be leashed at all times or shut up behind high fences. Dog owners disobeying the ordinance would be forced to clean up doggie-do personally, without tools. (It has been pointed out by some of the finer minds in town, that leash law or no, dogs will still do.)

Those people who love canines, and speak Dog at every opportunity, demand the council pass an ordinance that would require water receptacles to be placed on each street corner for meandering tailwaggers to drink from. Any human vandals knocking over, or drinking from, the dog dishes, especially in hot weather, would be confined on a leash in their homes and fed nothing but thin gruel for ten days.

The paper reports in full on the recurring dog controversy, but local political issues make the front page about once per year when electoral candidates buy space for their pictures along with five lines of copy admiring accomplishments. All other political news is found under "Sheriff's Report."

Even though you may be barely arrived and barely acquainted in your chosen small town, it is wise to subscribe at once to the local paper. Careful scrutiny of its columns will help you separate the black hats from the white, and the folks whose vital statistics are described within its pages are going to be your friends and neighbors. Without a weekly perusal of the "Express Review," you're doomed to remain a wallflower, conversationally speaking.

EDIFYING WOOLLY WEST EDICTS

Out West, who do you yell at after a snowstorm clogs the country roads?

Answer: The County Commissioners.

— ● —

In a Woolly West local paper, what headlines banner ahead of the Presidential election, war news or the eruption of an extinct volcano?

Answer: a) The victorious score of the basketball or football team.

b) Bagging a moose that has a record breaking set of antlers.

CHAPTER 26

WHEAT FROM CHAFF
(How to tell Westerners from Greenhorns and vice-versa)

You can tell a Greenhorn . . .

. . . by the way his hips are broader than his shoulders.

. . . because he appears in public without a hat or cap.

. . . because he wears short-sleeved shirts.

. . . his nails are clean and sometimes actually buffed and polished.

. . . he wears a tie for occasions other than funerals or weddings.

. . . he walks with his toes pointed outward.

. . . he wears open-toed sandals in the corrals.

. . . he wears Hawaiian shirts in public.

. . . he wears earmuffs in cold weather.

. . . his jeans stay new looking longer than 45 minutes.

. . . he doesn't know how to spit, chew or roll his own.

. . . he drinks Martinis.

You can tell a Woolly Westerner by the way . . .

. . . his hat sits so low on his face he has to tip back to see.

. . . his hat never leaves his head, especially in public places.

. . . he wears a wide belt with his name carved on it cinched below his stomach so his paunch has a place to rest.

. . . he wouldn't be caught dead in a short-sleeved shirt.

. . . his walk resembles John Wayne with arthritis.

. . . he never lowers the flaps on his winter cap till the temperature drops to 40 below.

. . . he never wears ties except to weddings and funerals (his own).

. . . his new jeans acquire an aged look within 15 minutes.

. . . he drinks beer or a ditch (whiskey and water). Cocktails are what birds have.

HOW TO GET SHOT AT OUT WEST

a. Drive on a rancher's irrigated hayfields.
b. Cut a rancher's fences.
c. Litter the river bank.
d. Ask fool questions.
e. Let your darling dog chase the livestock.
f. Let your darling dog kill the chickens, in which case the ranch woman will ventilate your form.

Out West, it is legal to shoot a dog that is trespassing or harassing sheep, cows, horses or other livestock. Little sympathy will be wasted upon you when the family pet shows up dead three miles down the road, where he went for his morning sheep-chasing frolic.

EDIFYING WOOLLY WEST EDICTS

What should you do when following in a vehicle behind a herd of cows, a band of sheep or possibly a flock of turkeys?

Answer: Do NOT honk.

• ● •

Is the man on foot following after the sheep and rattling a bunch of beer cans strung on a wire having a spiritual experience?

Answer: No. Nor is he having a seizure or executing a mysterious native dance. The shaking and rattling are maneuvers designed to remind lagging ewes to keep up with the bunch.

When the thoughtful can-rattler urges his charges to one side of the highway, that means you may drive past, **slowly.**

Do NOT honk.

• ● •

What do you do when forced to slow your car to a turtle pace behind a flock of sheep blocking the entire highway?

Answer: Refrain from debarking from your vehicle. Though your goal may be to separate the bunch like parting a woolly sea, remember if you're wearing sandals or possibly no footwear at all, walking behind a flock of woollies means trampling what looks like licorice-covered peanuts. They are not. These deceptive nuggets can squish up between bare toes, over the edges of sandals and can emanate odor no amount of Chanel No. 5 can conquer.

Do NOT honk.

• ● •

When approaching a bunch of cattle, do not move up to within a hair of the last animal so that the horseman can't maneuver behind the critters. Wait for the rider to lead you through. Follow his horse as you would a pilot car through a road-construction maze.

Do NOT honk goodbye.

The End